MORYA

**Dictations received through the Messenger
Tatyana Nicholaevna Mickushina
from 2005 through 2015**

2nd Edition

UDC 141.339=111=03.161.1
BBC 87.7 + 86.4
   M 59

M59 Mickushina, T.N.

Morya.

Masters of Wisdom. / T.N. Mickushina. –
2nd Edition. – 2016. – 242 c. – ("Masters of Wisdom" series).

This book continues the Masters of Wisdom series of books.

This series of books presents collections of Messages from different Masters who are most well-known to modern humanity. These Messages were transmitted through the Messenger Tatyana N. Mickushina, who has been working under the guidance of the Masters of Wisdom since 2004. Using a special method, T. N. Mickushina has received Messages from over 50 Beings of Light.

The present book contains selected Messages of Master Morya. Many Teachings are given in the Messages, including the Teachings about:

- actions in the physical plane,
- Service to Brotherhood,
- the attainment of the qualities of a disciple such as devotion, persistence, aspiration, and discipline

Some aspects of the Teaching about changing of consciousness are also introduced here.

ISBN 1523938048
ISBN-13: 978-1523938049

Contents

Master Morya 7

The moment has come for you to give up any
manifestation of conflict in your consciousness.
March 20, 2005 40

You have come into this world to act.
Perform your duty!
April 25, 2005 47

I will enter your temples and act through you.
April 28, 2005 54

You can receive at your disposal the mightiest
tool of God.
April 29, 2005 61

For those of you who are ready to follow the Will of God,
I will be a much more caring nurse than you would ever
be able to find in the physical plane.
May 5, 2005 67

Aspiration, constancy and devotion — these are
the qualities necessary for our disciples.
May 14, 2005 74

You must act, act and act.
May 21, 2005 81

Kindle your torches and set off to bestow your flame
to the world.
May 25, 2005 88

Russia is spring cleaning now.
June 9, 2005... 95

A Teaching on Freedom.
June 19, 2005 101

Your consciousness is the only restriction of your
Divine Freedom.
June 21, 2005... 103

I congratulate you on the successful completion of this
unique experiment on the transferring of the vital and
timely information to the physical plane.
June 30, 2005 110

Faith is the remedy that you need.
December 21, 2005 115

Instructions about your attitude to everything around
you in your dense world and in the finer worlds.
April 20, 2006 120

We are calling you to follow our Path.
April 30, 2006 126

There will be those who manifest their consistency and
devotion and can help us attain our goals.
July 7, 2006 131

Feel responsibility and keep your aspiration.
July 19, 2006 136

I wish you successful self-perfection.
July 21, 2006 140

We hasten to bring home to your consciousness
the new tasks which need implementing.
December 27, 2006 144

A Teaching on Devotion.
January 10, 2007 149

Exhortations for the current day.
June 22, 2007 153

**All your life must be devoted to
the Divine Service.**
July 10, 2007 159

A message to my disciples.
December 23, 2007 164

**I have come to inform you about the end of another
stage of our work and about the beginning of
the next one.**
January 10, 2008 169

**It is needed to go and perform the tasks of
the Brotherhood now.**
July 1, 2008 172

**The severity of the moment obliges me to warn you
about what is happening.**
December 29, 2008 176

**The time of training is over; the time is ripe for practical
classes in action yoga.**
January 5, 2009 180

**We continue the mission that we have started
in Russia.**
July 10, 2009 185

**I wish to instill confidence in you and liberate you
from fear.**
January 21, 2010 189

**We give our helping hand to everyone who asks
us for help.**
June 05, 2010 193

Not going wide but moving deep you reach.
December 23, 2010 197

An ability to admit.
June 26, 2011 202

I am clearly showing you the Path and the direction of your advancement.
January 2, 2012 207

It is necessary to start acting!
December 28, 2012 211

You must return God into your life!
December 27, 2013 217

Show your achievements and we will be ready to give you better understanding and more knowledge!
June 29, 2014 222

I hope that my Message will light up the hearts of those who still have a sparkle of Divinity glowing inside!
June 21, 2015 226

Right now it is the time for your work for the good of the evolutions of planet Earth!
December 23, 2015 230

Master Morya

Master Morya (Maurya or El Morya) is Mahatma,[1] a Teacher of the Great White Brotherhood, who became famous to the world due to the establishment of the Theosophical Society in the nineteenth century. Helena Blavatsky announced its existence in the 1880s. Masters Morya, Kuthumi, and Djwal Kul helped to found the Theosophical Society.

Throughout the period around 1920-1950, Master Morya was cooperating with Helena and Nicholas Roerich. Thanks to that cooperation, The Teaching of Agni Yoga or Living Ethics came into the world, which was given to prepare the consciousness of humanity for a new step of development, the acceptance of fire energies coming to the World.

In the 1960s, Mark and Elizabeth Clare Prophet were writing a lot about Master Morya. Many messages from Teacher Morya and other Masters came through the American Messengers.

---

[1] Mahatma (Sanskrit) – literally is a Great Soul. An Adept at the highest stage of Initiation. In pali language - Arhat.

In the beginning of the 21st century, the Masters continued their work through a Messenger in Russia, Tatyana Mickushina.

Now, Master Morya is still actively working on the Spiritual plane to help the humanity of the World.

This is what Helena Blavatsky told us about the Mauryas' dynasty.

"Maurya (Sanskrit) – one of the Buddhist royal dynasties of Magadha, to which Chandragupta and his grandson Ashoka belonged. It is also a name of the Radjput tribe."[2] "Chandragupta was the first Buddhist Monarch of the Maurya dynasty. Ashoka was the most diligent adherent of Buddhism; he kept from 60 to 70 thousand monks and priests in his palace; he erected 84 thousand stupas around India, and sent missions around the world. Texts of various edicts that he declared contain the most noble ethical ideas, especially the edicts of Allahabad written on the so-called 'Ashoka's column.' These texts are sublime and poetic; they express fondness for animals and for people, as well as an idealized view of the ruler's mission regarding his people. This view could be successfully followed in our days."[3]

"In the Buddhist *Mahavansha*, Chandagutt – Chandragupta a grandfather of Ashoka – was called the

---

[2] From *Theosophical Dictionary* composed by H.P. Blavatsky.

[3] Ibidem.

8

prince of the Maurya dynasty, whom he was undoubtedly, or to be more precise, whom they were, since there were several Chandragupta. This dynasty, as it is stated in the same book, started with some Kshatriyas (warriors) of the Shakya lineage, who were closely related to Gautama Buddha and who, having passed through the Himavat (the Himalayas), discovered a captivating land, well irrigated and located in the middle of the forest of the magnificent Bodhi and other trees. There they founded a city called Shakya Maurya—Nagar by its masters."[4]

It is known that in his last earthly incarnation, Morya was born as a Radjput prince in the Indian cast of warriors and rulers who were respected for their courage and dignity. His date of birth is not known precisely. His name was Ranbir Singh. In 1858, after his father's death, Ranbir became a maharajah of Kashmir. Historians appreciate Ranbir for uniting the Nagar and Hunsa states and establishing humane and fair civil and punitive laws. Ranbir was very popular among his countrymen. He passed away in 1885.

According to description, he was about two meters tall and had a military bearing. He spoke in a laconic way, as if he had been used to the thorough following of his directions. He usually wore white clothes and a turban. He gave an impression of a person in the prime of his life of about 35 years old; however, according to

---

[4] Puranas about the dynasties of Morya and Kuthumi from a book by H.P. Blavatsky, *The Himalayan Brothers*. Moscow: Sfera, 1999 (in Russian, unpublished).

Helena Blavatsky, when she saw the Master in London's Hyde Park in 1851, he looked exactly as he had in her childhood (Mahatma Morya had come to her in dreams since her childhood).

During that first meeting in London, the Master told H. Blavatsky that he "needs her for one of his future under-takings" and that "she will have to spend three years in Tibet in order to prepare for this important task."[5] Twenty-seven years later, Blavatsky came to India and Tibet, where she met the Master again.

Master Morya's life is notable due to his devotional work on uniting ancient verities of the East with traditions of the West. This task was fulfilled mainly through the foundation of the Theological Society in New York in 1875 and further teachings through that organization. Those teachings were received partly through private letters mailed to a handful of *Mahatma Gimavat's* disciples. Later, in 1923, the letters were collected and published under the title *The Mahatma Letters*. Certain chapters were translated into the Russian language by H.I. Roerich and published under the title *The Cup of the East* in Riga in 1925. *The Mahatma Letters* were published in their entirety in Russia in 1993. The originals of the letters are kept in the British Museum in London.

Helena Blavatsky stated that, thanks to Mahatmas Morya, Kut Humi, and other Masters, her major books,

[5] Wachtmeister C., *Reminiscences of H.P. Blavatsky and "The Secret Doctrine."* London: Theosophical Publishing Society; New York: *The Path*, 1893, Pages 56-58.

Isis Unveiled and *The Secret Doctrine*, which claim a common origin of all world philosophic systems and religions, were written.

In her book *Letters from the Caves and Jungles of Hindustan*, Helena Blavatsky described her journeys around India with her Master, whom she calls Gulab Lall Singh: "... an extraordinarily tall Rajput, an independent Thakur[6] from Rajasthan province; known by the name of Gulab Lall Singh, but everyone just called him Gulab Singh. ...about this person there were various rumors. Some of them were that he belonged to the sect of Raja-yogis, initiated in the secrets of magic, alchemy, and other clandestine sciences of India. He was a rich and independent man; no one even dared to suspect him of lying, especially because, even if he had been engaged in those sciences, he carefully kept his knowledge to himself and never shared it with anybody except his closest friends.

---

[6] "The Takurs of Rajputana, who are said to possess some of the underground libraries, occupy in India a position similar to the position of European feudal barons of the Middle Ages. Nominally they are dependent on some of the native princes or on the British Government; but de facto they are perfectly independent. Their castles are built on high rocks, and besides the natural difficulty of entering them, their possessors are made doubly unreachable by the fact that long secret passages exist in every such castle, secret of which is confided inheritably from father to son... No torture would ever induce the owners to disclose the secret of their entrances, but the Yogis and the initiated Adepts come and go freely". (A note from the book of H.P. Blavatsky *From the Caves and Jungles of Hindustan*.)

The Thakurs start their lineage from Surya (the Sun), which is why they are called Suryavansas, the offspring of the Sun, who never yield to anybody out of pride. There was a saying – 'earthly dirt cannot stick to the sun's rays, aka to the Rajputs.'"[7]

Let's bring up more examples from the book *Letters from the Caves and Jungles of Hindustan*, which tell more about the unique abilities of the Master.

"Taking up a lotus position on one of the benches, graven in a cliff at the very edge of a verandah, he was sitting motionless, embracing his knees with his hands and focusing his eyes on the silver distance. The Rajput was sitting so closely to the edge that any slight movement, it seemed, would have thrown him into the gaping abyss at his feet. But he moved no more than the standing across from him granite Goddess Bhavani... Only at times sparking flames of waning bonfires lit up his dark bronze face with a warm sheen, which allowed sometimes to see the motionless features on his Sphinx-like face as well as the burning coals that were his still eyes.

What is it? Is he sleeping or just remaining motionless? He is motionless, like motionless initiated Raja-yogi, whom he talked about in the morning... neither hissing, nor loud clock striking, nor my rapid movements... did not disturb Gulab Singha, who was

_____

[7] Blavatsky H. P. *From the Caves and Jungles of Hindustan.* London: Theosophical Publishing Society, 1892. Available at: http://blavatskyarchives.com/theosophypdfs/blavatsky_from_ the_caves_and_jungles_of_hindostan_1892.pdf.

still hovering over the abyss as before... A gust of pre-dawn fresh and rather strong wind rustled leaves all at once and soon all the tree tops sticking out from the abyss around us started sawing from side to side. All my attention was focused on the group of the three Rajputs sitting in front of me – on the two armor-bearers and their master. At that moment, I did not know why my attention was especially focused on the flowing long hair of the servants who were sitting on the veranda's side and were more protected from the wind than their master. A glance in his direction seemed to make the blood run cold in my veins – the wind was wagging a muslin veil strongly attached to a column back and forth; however, the master's long hair was running to his shoulders motionlessly, as if glued to them; not even a hair swayed; there was not even a slight movement in the folds of the muslin he was wrapped in; a statue could not look more motionless..."

That minute, a silhouette of a cat appeared on the platform. The tiger roared frightfully, perturbing all the travelers. Great turmoil arose. While men were obtaining rifles, the tiger disappeared from the platform, its body rolled into the abyss. As we found out later, Gulab Singh defeated the enormous wild cat with just a word.

In another chapter Blavatsky recalls how, together with two other fellow travelers, she went to examine caves, which were a chain of chambers going upwards many miles into the depth of the mountain. In one of the caves, she fainted from the shortage of air and was at risk of dying. Suddenly, from one of the upper caves, which the travelers had not reached yet, the

Master appeared, although he was supposed to be in another province at that time. "Gulab Singh came out of the upper cave with a torch in his hands and, jumping into the lower chamber, shouted to them to "hand" him "guab" (the sister)… Passing the half-dead burden from hands to hands, they hurriedly followed the Thakur; but Gulab Singh, according to their words, always managed to do without their assistance, despite all the difficulties caused by the 'baggage' (Helena Blavatsky was a rather corpulent woman – noted by the author). As they were crawling through the upper chamber, he was already at the next lower one, descending into the next cell, they could only see his white flying chador disappearing in the next exit. Thorough to pedantry, precise in his research, the colonel could not understand how the Thakur could carry the almost breathless body from passage to passage! … "How I was carried through five narrow passages will remain secret for me forever…" Let us note as well, that all Blavatsky's companions came out of the caves with faces and clothes covered with dirt and blood from multiple scratches; however, Thakur's clothes were still snow-white.

When the travelers were on a visit at Gulab Singh's house, a colonel discovered a picture there, which was engraved with a meeting of Rajput ambassadors. The picture was signed: "Drawn by Ahmed-Din in 1177 year" (or the year 1765 by Jewish chronology – author's note). On a parchment "…There was an image of takur Gulab Singh, standing by the throne of padishah, between 70 or 80 figures of royal Muslims and Brahmins!...a giant height of a figure superexalted it by head and shoulders above other figures, that was the only figure in the picture, absolutely free from menial pose of all other court nobilities…a figure of that person, at whom we all at once recognized Gulab Singh, risen high above the crowd, stroke eye by its prideful posture. Even the pose was his, peculiar to him only pose: he was standing with arms crossed on his chest, calmly looking over a distance over the head of court nobilities. Just his outfit was different…Long, wavy hair, a beard, a face didn't leave any doubt that it was him, our secret unexplainable favourer…" It appeared that 114 years ago Gulab Singh looked the same as at the time when he had accompanied Blavatsky and her companions in India.

Conceding to persistent requests of the colonel, by the end of the trip, Gulab Singh confessed:

"– I am indeed initiated into, what you call gupta-vidja – secret science…I am brahmacharya…[8]

What is 'secret science'?" – Thakur went on. "– To me this science, like to everyone who dedicated their lives to it, contains the key to all the secrets of nature, as well as visible and invisible worlds. But this key costs more than you think. Gupta-vidja is a double-edged weapon, which one cannot touch without sacrificing his own life or mind (which is even worse), as it defeats and kills everyone who does not manage to defeat it."

---

[8] A family line of laical monk, who was devoted to celibacy from the very birth and who had to learn siddhi – a science of theurgy, or white magic and thaumaturgics. (Note of H.P. Blavatsky in the book *From the Caves and Jungles of Hindustan.*)

Runbir Singh is the last earthly incarnation of Master Morya.

Different sources give different names of the last incarnation of Master Morya. Helena Roerich called the Master in this incarnation "raja Chernoya." Helena Ivanovna, Zinaida Fosdick, a closest collaborator of Roerichs in the U.S., writes in her diary: "...Akbar was incarnated as raja Chernoya; his astral body was injured, as he was always in public, in court events. He had always received pokes and injuries from all sides. It was necessary to come to the Brotherhood in a healthy physical body, which is why this incarnation is needed."[9]

Master Morya's earthly incarnations are numerous. They are mentioned in various sources: in Helena Blavatsky's work, in books and letters of Helena Roerich, in books by Mark and Elizabeth Prophet, etc.

Here we introduce the most famous incarnations of Master Morya.

Abraham (about 2000 BC).

He was a Jewish patriarch and a founder of Twelve Israelite Tribes. Jews, Christians, and Muslims consider him the first to worship the true one God.

---

[9] Fosdick Z.G. *My Teachers.* (Moscow: Sfera, 1998) 800p (in Russian, unpublished).

Abraham and his family were first mentioned in the Bible as citizens of Ur, a prosperous cultural, political, and economic center of Sumerian civilization.

Author Zecharia Sitchin states that Abraham was born in 2123 BC. He was a Sumerian aristocrat coming from a Greek family connected to the royal house by blood. The family had been rich, possessing numerous serfs and its own army.

The book Genesis depicts Abraham as a powerful ruler who associated with other rulers, entered military unions, and managed land properties. He loved peace, but was good at military science and generous as a victor. He was an embodiment of justice, purity, and hospitality. He is also depicted as a prophet and an intercessor before God. However, the most important is that Abraham is a prototype of a man who adheres to his faith in a reoccurring prophecy of God that he must become a "father of many peoples," even though external conditions suggest the opposite.

Genesis narrates that Abraham, together with his father and family, left Ur and settled down six miles outside of it, in Harran — a big trading center in the north-east of Mesopotamia, on the territory of present-day Syria.

Despite the fact that the Bible does not mention anything about the early period of Abraham's life, legends tell us that he participated in military campaigns, striving for the propagation of monotheism. People say that he shattered idols of his father Farrah, who, as it is stated in The Book of Joshua (24:2), worshipped "other gods."

In the Bible, it is said that when Abraham turned seventy-five years old and his father died, God called upon him to give up everything — his family, the home of his father, culture and cults of Mesopotamia — and set off on a journey to the land where He chose. God promised Abraham: "I will produce a great nation from you." Abraham left Harran, having taken with him his wife Sarah, his nephew Lot and "all the property which they had accumulated and all of their people in Harran." Upon arriving in the land of Canaan, God appeared to Abraham and said: "...unto thy seed I will give this land" (Genesis 12:5, 7).

During the famine, which befell on Canaan,[10] Abraham had to go south, to Egypt. After the hard times passed, Abraham returned back. He generously permitted his nephew Lot to settle in a fertile valley of

---

[10] Canaan – in Biblical times this was a country located on the West of the North-Western curve of the Euphrates and from Jordan to the shore of the Mediterranean Sea. Later an ancient country, Phoenicia, was located in this territory. It is currently split between Syria, Lebanon, Israel, and Jordan. Canaan is famous for being "The Land of Promise." God Yahweh promised to give these lands as a heritage to the descendants of Abraham. (Wikipedia, in Russian.)

Jordan. Abraham himself settled down on Canaan lands, which seemed the worst in Harran. God again told Abraham that He would give him and his offspring all the land seen "to the North, to the South, to the East, and to the West." Although the patriarch was still childless, God confirmed that Abraham's children will be countless, "counting your descendants will be as impossible as counting the dust of the Earth" (Genesis 13:14, 16).

At that time a war of four kings against five kings started. Victors took all the property of Sodom and Gomorra and captured Lot, who lived in Sodom, and took all his belongings. Having learned about it, the patriarch armed 318 people who had been born in house, and defeated enemies and freed Lot with all his property, as well as people and property of the king of Sodom. Having returned victorious, Abraham received blessing from Melchizedek – the king of Salim and a priest of the Supreme God. Melchizedek "brought out bread and wine," and Abraham gave him "a tenth of everything" (Genesis 14:18, 20).

In the Bible, Abraham also performs a role of a defender. God informed Abraham that he was going to destroy Sodom and Gomorra, which were wallowed in vice. Abraham took a promise from God that Sodom would remain undamaged if at least ten righteous men were found there. Nevertheless, the city was destroyed, but two angels had warned Lot about the coming disaster and he managed to escape death.

Despite the reoccurring promise of God to multiply Abraham's seed, after ten years spent in Canaan, Sara was still infertile. Following a custom of that time, she suggested to her husband that he would marry their servant Agar, so Agar would bear his child. Soon Agar gave birth to a son, Ismail. When thirty years passed and Abraham was ninety nine and Sara was ninety, God appeared in front of the patriarch as El Shaddai – God Almighty: "...to be your God and the God of your descendants after you" (Genesis 17:7, 19). He announced that this time next year, Sara would have a son Isaac and that Isaac — not Ismail — would become his father's heir. Exactly as God uttered, "Sarah became pregnant and bore a son to Abraham in his old age" (Genesis 21:2).

However, the patriarch's most difficult challenge was still ahead. God ordered him to sacrifice his only son

– the long-awaited heir — on one of the mountains on the land of Moriah. After a three-day pass, Abraham made an altar, put Isaac on firewood and raised his knife to inflict a strike to the boy. That very moment an angel of God called upon him: "... do not lay a hand on the boy. Do not do anything to him. Now I know that you fear God, because

you have not withheld from me your son, your only son" (Genesis 22:12). A ram was sacrificed to God and God ratified his promise with Abraham.

After Sara's death, Abraham married Keturah, who gave him six sons. Having provided for his sons, Abraham gave "all that he had to Isaac" (Genesis 25:5). Abraham died when he was 175 years old and was buried next to Sara in the cave of Machpelah, which is revered by Jewish people, by Christians, and by Muslims, – by everyone who counts their origin from Abraham.

Due to his strong ties with God and exemplary faith, Abraham, as it is noted both in Christian and Muslim scriptures, earned the right to be called a friend of God ("al-Khalīl" in the Koran, Second Chronicles 20:7, Isaiah 41:8). As apostle Paul said in the Epistle to the Romans, he is a father not only of Jewish people, but also "of all those who believe" (Epistle to the Romans 4:11). Muslims (those who claim that they originate from Abraham through Ismail) revere the patriarch more than other biblical figures. In the Old city in Jerusalem at Jaffa Gate there is a sign – an abstract from Koran: "There is no god but Allah and Abraham – His beloved one."[11]

Melchior (1st Century BC).

According to the Gospel of Matthew, the three Magi: Balthazar (an incarnation of Kuthumi), Melchior (an incarnation of Morya), and Caspar (an incarnation of Djwal Kul), came to the Jews of Bethlehem and presented

---

[11] Mark L. Prophet and Elizabeth Clare Prophet. *The Masters and their Retreats,* Corwin Springs, Montana: Summit University Press, 2003.

their gifts to the newborn baby Jesus: gold, frankincense and myrrh — gifts that were usually presented to Kings, Priests, and Prophets.

Arthur, King of England (5 AD).

King Arthur was a legendary leader of the Brits in the fifth century AD. He destroyed the Saxon conquerors and was the main character in a British epos and numerous chivalry novels.[12]

In the mythology of Old England, there is no period finer than the times of King Arthur's rule and his noble knights, when amidst gloomy Middle Ages there came a rise of nobleness and selfless devotion to the crown and the country. One can say that the era of King Arthur was the starting point of British history.

Exact dates of King Arthur's life are unknown; however, stories about his life are written down in history, as well as in legends of all Western Europe. The first mentioning of King Arthur is dated back to the sixth century, when King Uther Pendragon died without leaving an heir to the throne.

---

[12] Wikipedia.

According to other sources, King Arthur was the only son of the Great King of Britain, Uther Pendragon. Queen Igraine gave birth to her son Arthur, who was destined to become the great ruler of England. Perhaps, avoiding court intrigues, the birth of the royal heir was kept from the royal court. The boy was secretly given to Merlin the wise, an alchemist and magician, (an incarnation of Saint Germain) for fosterage. Merlin knew about the court intrigues and knew individuals who were daydreaming about seizing power and dethroning the legitimate heir. After Uther's death, Merlin revealed the 12-year-old (or the 16-year-old according to other sources) heir to the throne the secret of his birth and taught him the details of the art of war, which were to help Arthur conquer the country.

To solve the issue of who would become a new king, Merlin made a big square stone with a steel anvil appear in the yard of London Cathedral. A sword was struck into the anvil. There was a sign on the stone: "the one, who pulls the sword out of the anvil, is rightfully The king of all England."

"The test with the sword reveals the might of the soul free from the slave-like attachment to material objects. The stone and the anvil are the symbols of this soul. This is the evidence of the divine right of the kings – only the one who possesses the most prominent achievements in the consciousness of Christ deserves to rule..."[13]

---

[13] Mark L. Prophet and Elizabeth Clare Prophet. *The Masters and their Retreats*, Corwin Springs, Montana: Summit University Press, 2003.

Knights and warriors, kings and nobility, arrived from across the Western world, but only Arthur, a 12-year-old boy, could get the sword out. The archbishop of Canterbury crowned him the king of England.

In one of the combats with Sir Pellinore, Arthur broke the sword, which he got from the stone, and Merlin promised the king a new sword Excalibur, which was forged especially for him by the Elves of Avalon.[14] The Sword Excalibur had a power to slay without missing, but on one condition – to bare the blade only for a good cause and when the time comes, Arthur must return the sword to Avalon.

---

[14] In Celtic mythology, a paradise island in the Western seas.

Having become the king of Britain, Arthur married Guinevere (Gwenevere in other sources) – a daughter of King Leodegrance, whom Arthur had once saved. The newlyweds lived happily in Camelot.

During Arthur's noble rule, Britain enjoyed 12 years of peaceful life. In his court, Arthur gathered the bravest and the most devoted knights of the kingdom – Lancelot, Gawain, Galahad, Percival, etc. Different sources claim that the overall number of knights reached 100-150 people. For the knightly council, the Round Table was made, so nobody would feel either first or last and everyone would be equal among each other and before the king.

In the book *Ascended Masters and Their Retreats*, Mark and Elizabeth Prophet inform us that Knights of the Round Table and court mistresses were initiated disciples of the secret school of the Great White Brotherhood, continuing the traditions of the Pythagorean School in Crotone and Commune of Essenes in Qumran. They often revered and guarded the inmost verity of the Brotherhood, which Merlin, the court magus and king's advisor, had revealed to them. Knights' tournaments were a means to indicate the level of spiritual achievements of their souls.

Arthur led his knights in the search for the Sacred Grail – the cup from which Jesus drank at the Last Supper.

In the hot battle of Camlann, Arthur was mortally wounded. Then, according to the legend, three mysterious queens laid Arthur on a boat and took him to the island valley of Avalon.

According to some legends, the beautiful story of the noblest king of Medieval England is hardly over. At present, Arthur is just drowsing, ready to resurrect and save Britain in case of real danger. The epitaph on his grave in Glastonbury Cathedral reads: «Hic jacet Arthurus rex quandam rexque futurus» (Here lies Arthur, the king who was and the king who will be)[15].

Venerable Sergius of Radonezh (1314 – 1392).

Sergius of Radonezh is a saint of the Russian Orthodox Church, a founder of the monastery of Trinity (today Trinity Lavra of St. Sergius), and a reformer of the monkhood in Northern Rus'.

He was born in the city of Rostov (the Great) in 1314, during dark times for the Russian land, when it was suffering from the devastation by the Mongol Yoke. Baptized as Vorfolomej, this future defender of Rus' revealed miracles of holiness from birth. On Wednesdays and Fridays, the newly-born fasted and

---

[15] Arthur, the king of England. Vestnik Svetan (Messenger of Light) Available at: http://www.vestniksveta.ru/index/artur/0-11 (in Russian, unpublished).

refused his mother's milk. In his boyhood, he spent all his free time in prayers.

This is what Helena Roerich tells us about St. Sergius.[16]

From Venerable Sergius's biography we know that by his adolescence, he revealed characteristics of a hermit and a monk. Also we know about his meeting with an old man who clarified many signs to his parents, which accompanied their son's birth. The old man said that it is for their son "to become a home of the Holy Trinity in order to bring many to understanding of the Divine Testaments."

When Bartholomew (a baptismal name of St. Sergius – by the translator) was past adolescence and his matured body could tolerate the hardships of secluded living, he was able to fulfill his cherished dream.

Together with his brother Stephan in a dense forest, Bartholomew chose a hill which was called Makovets and was located not far from the river of Konchura. Later, the glorious monastery of Trinity appeared there. There the brothers settled down and built two log cabins, one for a church and another for living. This is how the powerful prophecy of the mysterious Schemamonk started to become true.

---

[16] Further material is composed based on the essay of N. Yarovskaya (H.I. Roerich) "St. Sergius of Radonezh" (in the collection *A colour of St. Sergius of Radonezh*, Publishing house: "Zviozdy gor" (Stars of Mountains), 2013 (in Russian, unpublished).

However, Stephan could not bear the hardships of the secluded life and left for another monastery. Bartholomew was left alone. At first, the old monk Mitrofan stopped by for worship services from time to time. Then days, months, and years of complete solitude passed. An emersion into a dismal silence of desertedness began. Undoubtedly, this was the hardest time, which required tremendous spiritual and bodily strength.

Rumors about his ascetic life were soon spread around and people began visiting him, seeking edification and advice in all life matters. The young ascetic let no one go without comforting words of approval and exhortation.

Finally, those who wanted to follow him in his heroism came to him and asked to be accepted as disciples. Sergius permeably examined their motives and souls. He never rejected those who sought heroism sincerely and only warned them about the hardships of secluded life and the fears that overwhelmed the newcomers.

When twelve disciples gathered at Sergius's and twelve cells were built, a tall fence was erected around the area. The fence had a gate and protected them from wild animals. The life of the hermits streamed peacefully in their newly-equipped Abode.

Venerable Sergius was an example of all possible labor and heroism – he carried water for the brotherhood, ground grains with a stone mill, baked the Hosts, made kvass, rolled church candles, tailored, and sewed clothes and footwear. He worked for the brotherhood, as Epiphanius the Wise said, "like a bought slave." In summer

 and winter, Sergius wore the same clothes; he was afraid of neither cold nor heat. Despite his malnourishment, he was very strong and "had strength against two people"; he was also tall. In services, he was the first. In between the services, he introduced into practice prayers in cells, labor in gardens, sewing, book rewriting, and even icon painting.

Numerous evidences of miracles that the saint performed were collected by witnesses. He resurrected the dead and healed the sick. The blind got their eyesight back just from a touch of his hand. When the monastery grew and had a shortage of water supply, after Sergius's prayer a powerful spring appeared not far from the monastery. The spring is still there and heals many people. Holy Virgin Theotokos and Mother Mary, together with two apostles, appeared in front of Sergius and counseled the ascetic saint.

After Venerable Sergius's death, the secluded life became widespread in Muscovite Rus'. The disciples and "interlocutors" of Venerable Sergius founded around forty monasteries of the new type, while the disciples of the disciples established sixty more monasteries. In the fifteenth and sixteenth centuries, all the forests in Northern Rus' were inhabited by hermits, spiritual children, and imitators of the Venerable Sergius. They developed agriculture, building construction, established trade, and made spiritual culture a foundation of state organization.

It can be said that the ascetic life of Sergius, who with his own example implemented a high moral teaching in life, demarcated the New Era in the life of the Russian land. Owing to the widespread establishment of new abodes and schools of strict ascetic life, the morality of the nation increased significantly. Whole settlements and suburbs, which appeared around such monasteries, were exposed to a constant example of elevated renunciation and selfless service to the neighbor.

When the Mongol army was about to attack Rus' again in 1380, Sergius blessed Prince Dmitry for the battle against a Tatar khan, Mamai, on the field of Kulikovo. Being able to foresee the future, Sergius predicted the victory of the Russian army.

In *Facets of Agni Yoga*, we read about Sergius: "He seized the turning point in the history of Russian Land and directed its flow in a proper direction, having taken the great responsibility for the outcome of the battle on Kulikovo field. He gave his blessing to Prince Dmitry and his army. He had to feel and understand the turning point and sacrifice his spiritual authority on the scale of history. And he did it... He actively participated in affairs of the Moscow state, helping the prince with his advice. His monastery was, so to speak, a spiritual center for the people seeking their liberation from the Tatar yoke.

Not in vain, Sergius was called a "Leader of the Russian Land."[17]

Venerable Sergius passed away when he was seventy-eight years old. When his coffin was opened thirty years after his burial, witnesses saw his imperishable relic, which exuded fragrance. Even the clothing of the deceased was unharmed, this despite the fact that the coffin had been in water for quite a while.

Venerable Sergius of Radonezh was a spiritual leader of the Russian people; indeed, according to Helena Roerich, he was "a creator of Russian spiritual culture."

Helena Roerich wrote: "...the essence of Sergius's life was not in exterior ecclesiasticism, but in his highly moral educational influence on his contemporaries. Setting strict regulations, he brought discipline into the wild temperaments of that time. He created a character of the nation, by which he established the might of the state. From history we know the chaotic condition in which the spirit of the nation was during the Mongol yoke and the rowdy temper of fighting against each other's princes. There was a need for a strict school and bridle, the means for which one had to get from the closest and most accessible concepts. There was a need for symbols. There was a need for formalism for the consciousness to grow out of its infant state. ...the memory of Sergius will never die, because great is the Magnet of the Spirit

---

[17] *Grani Agni Yogi* [*Facets of Agni Yoga*], Vol. 8, page 203. 12.04.1967 (in Russian, unpublished).

instilled by him in the soul of the Russian people. The history of the development of spirituality in the Russian soul and the beginning of unification and construction of the Russian land were tightly connected with this great ascetic."[18]

Akbar the Great (1542 – 1605).

Akbar, Jalal ud-din Muhammad (Akbar the Great) is the third shah in the dynasty of the Great Mughals, Timurid, a grandson of Babur, a direct descendant of Tamerlan.[19]

In the sixteenth century, the Mughal Empire in India was practically conquered by foreign invaders. In 1556, when Akbar Jalal ud-din Muhammad inherited the throne, only the capital city Delhi was left from the once vast empire. The outstanding young emperor, Akbar, who had not yet turned fourteen

---

[18] *Letters of Helena Roerich*, 1935-1939, 25 May 1936, Volume II. Available at: http://www.agniyoga.org/ay_pdf/ay_lohr2.pdf

[19] Tamerlan (Timur; 1336 – 1405) – one of the world's great conquerors, who played a well-marked role in the history of Middle, Southern, and Western Asia and Caucasus. A distinguished military commander, an emir (since 1370). A founder of the empire and Timurid dynasty with the capital in Samarkand. An ancestor of Babur – a founder of the Empire of Great Moguls.

by his coronation, on the moment of his coronation, set off to win back his empire. He became known in the entire world as Akbar the Great – the mightiest of all Mughal emperors.

Emperor Akbar had outstanding physical endurance, which contributed in his extraordinary military success. He could cover 240 miles (386 kilometers – noted by the author) riding a horse in 24 hours in order to catch the enemy off guard. The majority of his long rule was focused on conquering insurgent princes of northern India and facilitating peace by means of setting up strong local principalities.

Akbar extended the borders of his state, having conquered northern Hindustan, including Kashmir, Gujarat, and the lands of the Hindus river. He proved to be not only a good military leader and a brave warrior, but also a wise politician who tried to avoid bloodshed whenever possible and achieve results through peaceful negotiations, alliances, and marriages between dynasties.

In 1574, having finished the overall territorial formation of his state, Akbar began domestic reforms. The creation of a powerful centralized state on the basis of justice and equality among its inhabitants was a goal of these reforms. First of all, he reinforced control over the army, carried out a new administrative division of the state, and established a unified tax system. The tax reform was based on strict accounting rules, which prevented officials from appropriating and embezzling tax money. Alongside the tax reform, a law was passed not to tax people in times of bad harvest and famine and to give both money and grain loans. Akbar abolished this tax on the grounds that it was against Islam and that it humiliated the Hindu people. Throughout the empire, a unified length and weight measurement system, as well as a single solar calendar (based on the data of Ulugbek's tables) were adapted. The shah attached particular significance to trade, even as much as the Europeans. Trying to expand the supremacy of the Mughal Empire in India and to win the Hindu people over, Akbar assigned important positions in the state and the army to Hindu rajas.

Akbar also encouraged science and art and gathered the best scientists, poets, musicians, and artists around. His closest associate, vizier Abu al-Fazal ibn Mubarak, had a well-rounded education and spoke many languages. He compiled notes about Akbar's rule. During Akbar's reign a school of art was created and a vast library was collected, including more than twenty four thousand volumes. In 1569 on the outskirts of Agra the construction of a new capital, Fatehpur Sikri (the city of Victory), began. Soon it became a prosperous cultural center of India, larger than contemporary London.

Akbar's main task was to reconcile the various peoples who inhabited his growing empire. Treating all citizens equally, he permitted practice of all religions. In the new capital, a beautiful building with a majestic dome was built. It hosted disputes of religious topics, in which Akbar himself took active part. Together with Abu al-Fazal, he developed foundations of the so-called "divine faith," which combined elements of Hinduism,

Zoroastrianism, Islam, and, partly, Christianity. Akbar used to say: "Only believe that which is true, which is approved by reason." He wanted to show that there is only one true God, and that the various religions are simply different paths to approaching Him. At court, a special department was organized. The department did translations of various religious texts in order to show people the commonness of all religions, so people could give up hostility and fanaticism. He used to say: "Many fools, fanatics of traditions, accept customs of their ancestors as a manual of reason and, thus, doom themselves to shame." Akbar pointed out many barbarous customs, such as early marriages, self-immolation of widows, etc. Trying to establish the "divine faith" as a new religion, common for all of India, Akbar never forced anyone to follow any religion. He always relied on reason and people's free will. Tolerance was his distinctive feature. He never supported either cults or customs, believing that "one must serve God through pure deeds and thoughts."

However, as it has often happened in the history of humanity, it is the best undertakings that cause misunderstandings and implacable hostility. In 1580-82, a rebellion of prominent feudalists against Akbar's reforms broke out. The main moto of the rebels was "dethronement of the ruler – backslider." The stagnant consciousness of the zealots could not accept the politics of tolerance and brotherly attitude to representatives of other religions. The rebellion was defeated.

Akbar passed away in 1605, having been head of the state for fifty years. Under Akbar, the vast empire reached a glory which it never saw, before or after him. Akbar's constant care determined the wealth and prosperity of the country. When Akbar's son Jahangir inherited the throne, he rejected his father's reforms, especially regarding religious tolerance, and the empire quickly disintegrated. Akbar's grandson, Shah Jahan (Master Kuthumi's incarnation) inherited only a small out-of-control kingdom. However, he nourished great love to the cultural heritage of his grandfather. The greatest of the Mughal builders, Shah Jahan gave India the Taj Mahal, and with it a love story that is most dear to the hearts of Indians.

Akbar's following words sound like a conclusion to his life: "I am happy because I could apply the sacred Teaching to life, could give prosperity to people and overshadow enemies." He is remembered in history under the name of Akbar the Great – a wise ruler who united nations and whose idea of unity of all religions has survived centuries.[20]

Elena Ilina
Irina Koroteyeva

---

[20] Based on materials *Akbar II.* Mark L. Prophet and Elizabeth Clare Prophet. *The Masters and their Retreats,* Corwin Springs, Montana: Summit University Press, 2003.

We are giving the guidelines.
We are giving the basics.
We are giving the instructions.
For those who can hear.
For those who can acknowledge.
For those who are ready.

Master Morya

The moment has come for you to give up any manifestation of conflict in your consciousness

March 20, 2005

I AM El Morya! I HAVE come!

Beloved, have you recognized me? Lend your ear to my vibrations. There is something dwelling beyond all the words and images, and this something is Divine Reality which cannot be mistaken for anything else.

I have come from this highest reality to give you the following Teaching.

During the time of my last incarnation, I was known to you as El Morya. I came aiming to give the disciples in the West that part of secret knowledge which had been possessed only by initiated people since the times of the ancient Lemuria and Atlantis. The access to this knowledge was open only to a few initiated people, incarnated again and again with the aim to keep the flame of the Truth burning in this physical octave.

The Fire of the True Knowledge has never burned out, but it was accessible only for a very small circle of people who have always thoroughly guarded this knowledge from neophytes and laymen.

We, the three tsars El Morya, Kuthumi, and Djwal Kul, were incarnated in the 19th century and got an opportunity to share a part of the secret knowledge that had been possessed only by the highest initiated people on this planet. We managed to create the organization the "Theosophical Society" to spread this knowledge.

Due to the negative attitude of the West to everything coming from India and Tibet as being a lower knowledge in comparison with the knowledge possessed by the best minds of that age, we had to act through mediators capable of receiving and transmitting images and knowledge contained in our physical minds. Such a mediator who received information was Helena Blavatsky, our faithful disciple and follower. We also used a few people from the English aristocracy to spread our ideas.

A series of books was written under our dictation. We proofread thoroughly all the information which was to be published in order to explain the Truth as well as possible. And in fact all works given by us through Blavatsky contained the Truth, but the form of the given material was intentionally complicated. Therefore, the use of this Truth was possible only for those souls in embodiment that were given the necessary keys for its identification.

Our task was fulfilled brilliantly. We left on Earth the material evidence of the ancient Truth in the shape of

Blavatsky's printed works, though the true authorship of these books was certainly ours.

And we achieved the set goal. The creative thought of the best western minds was given the right direction. And the seeds of knowledge we had sown managed to germinate in many esoteric doctrines of the following century.

We were not able to give our Teaching in Russia. This country was the most receptive to receiving this knowledge. But exactly because of this fact all attempts were undertaken from the side of our opposition not to let this knowledge be available to Russians. Thus, the dissemination of our Teaching in Russia was delayed for a whole century. And when it finally came to Russia, this knowledge had already been diluted and made dull by many other Teachings born on the ground of America.

And even though the knowledge presented in our works and published through Blavatsky was on the basis of these esoteric Teachings, the distortions typical of the American mindset were still inherent in these Teachings to a significant extent.

At the moment of giving the knowledge we deliberately muddled the information so as not to reveal the Truth to unprepared minds. But in the new Americanized doctrines the Truth was already diluted by lies without our slightest wish.

These Americanized surrogates have finally reached Russia. And their only benefit was in the fact that people took up reading Blavatsky's works, for the authenticity of which we were personally responsible as we had participated in the creation of these books ourselves.

However, the minds of our sincere disciples were confused by the contradictions between new Americanized doctrines and the doctrines we had given.

As the new doctrines were given in a simple and clear language, exactly these new doctrines were preferred by our disciples and followers.

But the time has come when an insistent need has arisen to clear up the main contradiction. And it touches on the subject of the downfall of the angels and the question of Lucifer's downfall.

Last year we attempted to give a more simple explanation of the downfall of the angels and mankind through our messenger Tatyana, explaining and clarifying the description of these subjects given earlier in *The Secret Doctrine* by Blavatsky.

And now I have to return to this subject again as we see that this subject has come to the fore for our best disciples.

That is why we insist on your more attentive studying of this subject precisely as it is given in *The Secret Doctrine.*[21]

---

[21] Tatyana N. Mickushina, *Good and Evil, An individual interpretation of "The Secret Doctrine" by Helena P. Blavatsky.* Available from amazon.com/author/tatyana_mickushina

The moment has come for you to give up any manifestation of conflict in your consciousness including the fight with fallen angels.

In fact, two points of view, two approaches to mankind's history and to the conception of the universe's evolution, clash at this point. On the one hand, it is the approach typical of eastern philosophy and having found its reflection in the religious systems of India and Tibet. On the other hand, it is the approach inherent in western consciousness and borrowed from the ideology peculiar to the western Christian thought and new Americanized doctrines mentioned above.

Being geographically situated between the East and the West, Russia has a potential to absorb and master both philosophic systems.

That is why we have come again through a Russian Messenger to direct your thought.

The subjects of the downfall of the angels and the so-called rebellion of Lucifer are explained best of all in the works we wrote during our incarnation.

That is why the time has come to re-evaluate the knowledge given in the past and to raise your idea about the Truth to a new level.

Every time you have a wish to fight with fallen angels, remember that each of you has such an angel as the so-called fifth principle or Christ Self.[22]

---

[22] Tatyana N. Mickushina, "The fall of angels," in *Good and Evil, An individual interpretation of "The Secret Doctrine" by Helena P. Blavatsky.* Available from amazon.com/author/tatyana_mickushina

You cannot fight with a part of yourself. Your task is to help this fallen angel to come back Home to God.

But your four lower bodies, burdened by your karma's loads which you have accumulated during many embodiments on Earth, prevent him from doing so.

That is why all efforts should be directed to giving up the unreal part of yourselves, your ego, your karma's accumulations, and to raising your consciousness to the level of your Christ Self and your Guardian-Angel. It is the next stage of evolution and it will take place irrespective of how strongly you resist and stick to any system, offered to you kindly, but always leading you to the path of struggle.

Recollect the Teachings of Christ and Buddha. Did they teach you to fight with fallen angels?

Read the Bible again. Even in this source, though not pure enough from our point of view, you can find a correct conception of the history of Earth's evolution if you read these quotations with the help of the keys given in "The Secret Doctrine."

We spent a lot of effort and energy in order to overcome the resistance of Tatyana's external consciousness, to overcome any respect for the previous messengers, and to overcome the ideas about fallen angels given through these messengers from America.

That is why I speak through this Messenger while there is an opportunity to speak through her. And I confirm that times have changed, and it is necessary for you to rise to a new level of understanding of the Divine Truth.

You may choose. You may speculate. But do not forget that there are cosmic deadlines. And those who fail to meet these deadlines will swallow road dust.

I AM El Morya Khan.

You have come into this world to act. Perform your duty!

April 25, 2005

I AM El Morya, having come to you through this messenger again.

I hurry up with the fixing of my impetus of Light in Tatyana's force field. In accordance with the responsibility granted to me, I have been performing the procedure of anointing all the messengers during the last hundred years.

And now at this very moment I am placing my electronic presence over Tatyana as a sign of my patronage.

I have no opportunity to render sponsorship to any organization as there is no such organization in the physical plane. There is only a messenger there.

Therefore, I establish my sponsorship and fix a protective thread in Tatyana's aura from this day.

I am doing it now.

We did it!

From this moment I endow Tatyana with the powers to represent me in the physical octave and I take her under my patronage.

I am happy to have my representative in the physical plane of planet Earth again.

You know that I aspire to cooperate with people. There is no other Master having as many disciples as me. But I render my personal sponsorship very rarely and only in exceptional cases.

You may probably not guess what this means.

As soon as the Brotherhood receives an opportunity to enjoy a permanent focus of Light anchored in the aura of a messenger living in any country, not only this messenger but the whole country is taken under our protection while this focus of Light is active.

That is why I focus your attention on today's event. We will see what the future events will be and to what extent our hopes and confidence will be justified.

This concerns not only the messenger, but also the light-bearers embodied in Russia now. This is a chance for all of you to receive unprecedented support and help from the Heavens in all of your initiatives.

From now on I promise those of you who have accepted our messenger in your hearts to respond to any of your calls. I will give you all the help that can be given in all your undertakings. The only condition is the purity of your motives and the correspondence of your initiatives to the Will of God.

Beloved, are you aware of the opportunity you are being granted? Isn't it breathtaking to receive help and protection from the Ascended Hosts at the first call?

Can you imagine those fast changes which will take place around you?

Thus, all you need to do is to approach an altar or descend into your heart and make the following call:

"In the name of I AM THAT I AM, in the name of my Mighty I AM Presence, in the name of my Holy Christ Self and in accordance with the opportunity granted by beloved El Morya through the Messenger of the Great White Brotherhood Tatyana Mickushina, I ask the Will of God to be manifested in my actions which I perform in the name of God in this physical octave."

Further on you must set forth the essence of the undertaking or business in which you want to be helped by me personally or by the Ascended Hosts.

You may write down your request on a sheet of paper and then burn it. Thus, even lacking an organization, you are helped in your Divine deeds and the help is rendered to you directly, wherever you are.

It does not matter whether you act by yourself or together with a group of like-minded people.

In order to make use of the calls of the messenger and thus to have additional help in your business, I recommend that you transmit a copy of your request directly to my messenger.

From this day Tatyana receives the mantle of my personal messenger in addition to the mantle of the Messenger of the Great White Brotherhood which was laid on her shoulders a year ago.

Thus, we will soon know all the light-bearers who are ready to join this new dispensation and to act in its framework.

However, this dispensation differs from the previous ones. Earlier we anchored the focus within a certain organization in a certain country. As a rule, a messenger was at the head of such an organization and had to shoulder all the work of the organization. At present we have chosen another way. At your request we will render sponsorship to the organizations which you will found in your localities.

Don't wait for any commands except behests of your heart.

You were embodied, and each of you came into embodiment with a certain mission. And you know what you are to do.

It is not necessary for you to found an organization embracing all the aspects of activity. Moreover, the organization does not have to be social or religious.

50

You may found a commercial organization in order to affirm the Divine principles in the methods of conducting business in your countries. You may start your own public-health institution or any educational institution.

The only demand for you is to view the Divine principles as a priority in your activity, to lay them in the basis of your organization, and to help the people around you.

Don't strive for money. You will have exactly enough money for the implementation of your plans.

Money and the energy of money are only a secondary factor. The most important factor is the purity of your hearts and your wish to fulfill the Will of God.

This is the service that you have come to carry out in this world. The time for concrete actions has come. And don't tell me that you don't know what to do. Look around you.

Don't your eyes see the things for which your abilities, your efforts, hands and feet can be used?

The time for concrete actions has come. You have come into this world to act. Therefore, be so kind as to perform your duty.

You have had enough idle talk and discussing which of you have achieved bigger results on the Path. I want to see what you can really do in the surrounding physical world.

You have come into this world to act. Perform your duty!

If you still have not understood what I am talking about, I will have to descend to you, roll up my sleeves and show you what you ought to do.

Look how much rubbish there is around you.

And this is not only physical rubbish. This is the rubbish overfilling your mass media, TV, radio, Internet, and newspapers.

Clean up the rubbish around you and inside of your consciousness.

If some of you do not know what to apply your efforts to, nothing is left for you but to pray and ask God for enlightenment, because you have torn yourselves away from the Divine Reality and cannot even realize the distance between your world and the world of the Divine Reality.

Times have changed, and now after the change of the cycles we are choosing another way of acting.

We will not found a united organization which can become a tasty morsel and a temptation for the people who desire to rule.

No, we will place our focus of Light over any organization which will address us directly or through this messenger and ask for our patronage and which will meet our principles. We will act through each one who has prepared his temple for our coming. We will simply accept your invitation to enter your temples and take up your proposal to become our hands and feet in the physical plane.

And we will enter your temples. It will take place so naturally that you will not even notice our presence, and we will show you the best path to follow and the foremost task to apply your efforts.

If one of you says that he has no opportunity to found his own organization, to start his own business, or that he is lacking like-minded people and supporters and is absolutely lonely, let me not believe it.

You live among people, and these people need your help. You have four lower bodies, and these bodies need to be purified.

Therefore, don't tell me that you do not know what to do and what to occupy yourselves with.

The time for the active deeds has come. You will be rendered help from the Heavens in all of your endeavors if they correspond to the Will of God!

What are you still waiting for?

Shall I really come to you and show you what to do? Then hold up your shoulders, and I will shift off a part of my duties and a part of my work on to you.

Everyone should do his business. Start working and you will be astonished with the help that you will be given.

I AM El Morya, and I am always with you wherever you perform your concrete deeds in the name of God.

I will enter your temples and act through you

April 28, 2005

I AM El Morya, having come to you again through my messenger.

I HAVE come to you to affirm new knowledge and understanding of the events taking place in the higher plane of planet Earth now.

You know that the cycles are changing now. Many words were told about that, both in the dictations given through this messenger and in the dictations given by us through other messengers.

What characterizes the present stage of the transformations happening on Earth now and connected with the changing of the cycles?

You will be surprised if I tell you that the transformations in the higher plane have been practically completed. All the layers of the higher plane, with the exception of the lowest astral layers, have been purified by us from those negative energies which managed to penetrate to the layers that were not inherent in their essence.

It was grandiose work, beloved, and it has been completed by us effectively.

Now the phase has come when we start, properly speaking, purifying the layers close to the physical plane and purifying the very physical plane as well.

What is the difficulty? The forces that managed to penetrate illicitly to the layers with high vibrations are now pressed down to Earth by us. And they look for any pretext to strengthen their positions in the physical plane and in the densest layers of the astral plane.

These forces do not have their own source of the Divine Energy, and they feed on your energy which you grant at their full disposal so thoughtlessly at times.

Therefore, the question of the checking of the spending of the Divine Energy appears in the foreground now. The motive of almost all these dictations, if you reread them attentively, is just the control over the expenditure of the Divine Energy which you, beloved, must perform by yourselves.

Each of you is a source of the Divine Energy for your physical world. You choose yourselves — as the creatures endowed with the free will — where to spend the Energy granted to you by God.

It is impossible for you not to spend this energy. Every minute and every second of your living on Earth, the Divine Energy comes into your aura as a continuous flow from the Divine world. And it depends only on you, how you will use your Divine Energy.

The forces of darkness do not have access to the Divine Energy, but they are very experienced in the tricks of misappropriation of your Divine Energy. They take the energy you grant them so thoughtlessly through any non-divine actions that you let yourselves perform in your world.

The entire modern industry devotes 90% of its activity to satisfying the energetic needs of the forces of darkness. Have you ever thought about it, beloved? It seems harmless to you to go to a concert of rock music, to see horror films, soap operas, and films contributing to the violence propaganda.

It seems inoffensive if you, following fashion, buy things which are absolutely unnecessary for you. Each thing that you buy contains certain vibrations inside of it. There are things bringing the Light, and there are things taking your Light from you. Do you think about this when you spend your money — an equivalent of your Divine Energy — on the purchasing of non-divine things?

Do you ask for advice of your Christ Self when making your purchases?

Every moment of your life you make a choice, and this choice directs your Divine Energy either onto the multiplication of the illusion of this world or onto its contraction.

You tint your Divine Energy with beautiful feelings full of joy and love, and you raise the vibrations of this world. But when you are full of negative thoughts and feelings, you fill this world with heavy energy, viscous treacle of your negativity.

Only you can establish control over every erg of the Divine Energy spent by you. We cannot do it for you. We desire each of you to turn into an electrode of Light, filling the world around you with the vibrations of harmony, beauty, love, and joy. And we undertake a responsibility to help each of you who will truly want to help us in our work on the purification of your octave from the forces of darkness. But we cannot force you to make your choice, beloved.

We offer you a very simple decision, not requiring of you any additional time that is usually necessary for prayer-reading, though the prayers are now necessary as never before, being an extra source of Light for the physical octave. But if you constantly keep control over yourself and over the spending of your Divine Energy, it will not require any extra expenditure from you. On the contrary, it will help you save your financial resources. If you think over the question of where you spend your money, it will be clear that 90% of the things and food which you purchase are absolutely unnecessary for the maintenance of your physical body. On the contrary, they help to ruin your body, and you become dependent on the whole industry which involves you first into the process of the destruction of your physical body and your psyche, and then courteously offers you an immense set of expensive methods by which you can restore your health.

Keep control over yourself during the day. Watch your thoughts and your feelings. Your thoughts give the direction for the flow of your energy. Analyze what you think about. If you think about the unjust government, then you send your energy to the members of your government. If you think about your boss mistreating you at work, then you send him your energy. If you think about the plot of the soap opera you watched before, then you send your energy on the multiplication of the whole egregore of artificial thoughts and feelings in the astral plane.

You are responsible for every erg of energy wasted by you thoughtlessly. Every time you waste your energy not in accordance with the Divine principles, you create karma. And if you are aware of the karmic law but still go on violating the Divine principles to please your ego, your karma's character becomes much heavier.

Believe me; we never say our words without a purpose. And we do not spend our energy in vain. Every word told in these dictations through this messenger is directed exactly toward giving you the knowledge which you need most at this moment.

That is why we do not become tired of repeating to you one and the same thing: you are responsible for the spending of your energy, and you are twice as responsible for the spending of your energy if you continue your way of life after reading these dictations and persuade yourself that nothing told in them concerns you in any way.

You are in embodiment in the physical octave, and before being embodied many of you undertook upon yourselves the duties of helping mankind in this hardest time of the changeover. Now we remind you about the responsibilities undertaken.

Do not say then, when you appear in front of the Karmic Board, that you knew nothing and guessed about nothing, that you were not warned and you heard nothing.

I repeat it to you again and again. You have run out of time for learning. You are required to perform concrete actions and concrete steps in the physical plane.

It is hardly possible to formulate our demands to you more clearly than was done through this messenger. You should alter the priorities of your consciousness.

Remember, that we are powerless to do anything in your physical plane without your help and support. We have no access to your physical world, unless some of you prepare your temples for our presence and ask us to use your four lower bodies so that we can use your hands and feet for the implementing of our plans.

Thus, I give you this appeal. Please, make it every day.

"In the name of I AM THAT I AM, in the name of my mighty I AM Presence, in the name of my Holy Christ Self, I appeal to beloved El Morya to enter my temple and act through me so that the Will of God can be manifested in the physical octave and in the densest layers of the astral plane. Beloved El Morya, I grant all my four lower bodies at your full disposal: the physical body, the astral body, the mental body

and the etheric body. Act through me if there is God's Holy Will for that. Let God's Will be done. Amen."

I promise to you that as soon as an opportunity occurs I will enter your temples and act through you.

And thus we will change this world! And the Earth will live and become a beautiful star of liberty, joy, and love!

I AM El Morya, and I have given this message from the point of the highest Love towards you.

You can receive at your disposal the mightiest tool of God

April 29, 2005

I AM El Morya, having come to you!

I HAVE come to give you a small Teaching connected with the opportunity you acquire when all of your four lower bodies and your chakras become pure.

You know that the four lower bodies of most people living on Earth now are in an extremely impure state.

And as far as you know that your chakras link your lower bodies among themselves and with the Divine world, it means that your chakras are also a very sorry sight.

Therefore, today I intend to give you a certain Teaching connected with the opportunities that you acquire when your chakras are pure.

There are abstract talks about the purification of your four lower bodies and about the purity of your chakras, but this will sound more practical for you.

Thus, your chakras. You know that you have seven major chakras located along the spinal column, and you also have the secret rays' chakras, located along the spine as well, and you have many more chakras focused in many parts of your body. You know that there are a total of 144 chakras.

Twelve chakras transmit the perfect God-qualities to your world through the 12 Cosmic Rays, and each of these qualities bears in itself 12 more shades or half-tones.

When your chakras open like fascinating flowers, you become conductors of the perfect God-qualities into your physical reality.

God foresaw in advance all of the possible abuses that mankind could carry out by wasting the Divine Energy. Therefore, when you misuse the Divine Energy from the point of view of the Divine Law governing in this universe, this affects first of all the capacity of your chakras. The Divine Energy flowing into your bodies along the crystal cord is limited naturally. This resembles a tap through which the Divine Energy streams into the physical world and which is first slightly turned off and finally turned off completely. And your possibilities of abusing the Divine Energy are cut down.

That is why the state of consciousness inherent in mankind at the present stage of its evolution cannot have at its disposal the unlimited Divine might. It is because the first thing your consciousness would do, having received access to the unlimited source of the Divine Energy, would be to misuse this energy for satisfying the needs of its ego.

But you know that the needs of your ego are impossible to satisfy. They are limitless. Therefore, the access to the Divine Energy is reliably closed for most of mankind.

In order to receive access to the Divine Energy you have to choose the Path of Initiations. This Path lasts for not only one life. In exceptional cases, and only for our selected chelas, we allow this Path to be passed during one life.

You are given tests or trials for each of the God-qualities. And you must pass each of these tests 12 times. You have to pass 144 tests in total for the successful finishing of the initiations on the 12 chakras, which is necessary for them to be open.

If it were not for the returning tests which you have to pass due to your negligence, you could have achieved success during just a few years.

What does the opening of your chakras give you? Why do you need to aspire to it?

A person having at his disposal such a mighty tool as open chakras can provide the world with invaluable service. The major part of this service is in the purification of the surrounding world from any negative vibration and negative energies.

The might of your chakras is able to neutralize an utterly unimaginable quantity of the falsely qualified energy that your world is literally saturated with.

When you, beloved, utter your decrees or prayers, you attract additional Light into your world. This Light goes into your world through your chakras. Now imagine how much more Light you would be able to conduct into your world if your chakras were fully open.

But at the moment when all your chakras are open you will have become a perfect Buddha — that is, you reach the level of consciousness of Buddha in your own consciousness. Then, you cannot admit even into your thoughts anything that can do the slightest harm to the world or the living creatures around you.

You are constantly in the praying state of consciousness. But you do not even have to utter the words of your prayer in order to stay in the praying state of consciousness all the time.

At times, your chakras even work independently of your consciousness like a vacuum cleaner, drawing into them all of the rubbish from the world around you and filling this world with an irreproachably pure Divine Energy.

Therefore, when your chakras are open, you can appeal to your I AM Presence by asking it to direct the energy of your chakras for resolving this or that situation in your world. If your asking is in correspondence with the Law of God, then your I AM Presence will run the work of your chakras itself, and the energy will be directed to the concrete situation that you ask about in your appeal.

You can use the energy of your throat chakra to protect yourself and also to protect all those whom you have the right to protect in accordance with God's Law.

You can transmute the karma with help of your chakras, not only your own karma, because by that moment you will not have your personal karma, but the karma of the planet and of the country. You may give your direct help to the people who need it and who ask you for help.

This means actually fantastic opportunities and invaluable help to mankind, which you can give if you pass the necessary initiations for the opening of your chakras.

In order to understand better the might which comes to your disposal in this case, I will give you the following example.

Ten minutes of pulsation of your central chakra transmuting the karma will substitute for the uttering of the violet flame decrees during 400 hours.

This is really the mightiest tool, beloved, and this tool is hidden inside of you.

Today's talk was aimed at revealing to you the perspectives and opportunities of the next step.

Beloved, many of you are ready for this step and many are halfway to the full opening of your chakras.

You should know what to aspire to and what is your next step. You will receive at your disposal the might which is under the absolute control of your I AM Presence. If you attempt to use this might not in accordance with the Will of God, your chakras simply will not pulsate. But, if you still find a way to get around the Cosmic Law and to use the Divine Energy for your own purposes, your chakras will close and you will be refused access to the Divine Energy in the visible future.

God is ready to give you the most perfect tool, so necessary for you at this difficult time for planet Earth. Take it. Use it. It depends only on you, beloved, whether you will or will not receive this perfect tool at your disposal.

I tell you: The time has come; you can receive this mightiest tool of God at your disposal.

You only need to make a choice, to aspire to the Path of Initiations, and to pass with honor each of the initiations that God will let you pass.

I AM El Morya, and I will meet you on the Path of Initiations.

For those of you who are ready to follow the Will of God, I will be a much more caring nurse than you would ever be able to find in the physical plane

May 5, 2005

I AM El Morya, having come to you through my messenger again.

The tension of the recent days will not delay affecting the situation in the world. The currents of the space are tense. Do you feel this tension? You cannot help feeling it.

The reality around you, everything which seemed to you familiar before, seems unfamiliar and strange now. The change of the earthly vibrations is perceived by you as a lack of correspondence, as a disparity between you with your feelings and everything around you.

It seems as if everything is the same, but it is somehow amiss, not quite right. And there is no explanation of what is going on in the physical plane and in your consciousness. Your scientists try to explain the events on Earth with the help of their devices, which now give such unusual readings as have never occurred during the entire course of existence of the modern science.

Yes, beloved, when mankind clashes with the implementing of God's Plans, it has no choice but to submit to the Will of God. The cycle of plunging into the matter has been going on too long and you have gotten used to the fact that the matter obediently realizes your thoughts and wishes, and it obediently reflects them like a mirror. But now something has changed.

There are periods when mankind is allowed to experiment, but then the time comes and the situation changes. Neither you nor all your scientists are able to explain what is happening on the planet. There is something which in no ways submits to the will of the people. If God has planned the change of cycles for planet Earth, then this will be implemented independently of your wish.

The time has come to submit to the Will of God. There is the Law of this universe and this Law will be observed whether you wish it or not.

That is why I insistently recommend that you determine in your heart what in your life goes on in accordance with the Will of God for the given stage of the earthly evolution and what in your life is in conflict with the Will of God.

I realize that in your consciousness it is hard for you to differentiate your own wishes and aspirations from the Will of God for your lifestream. However, the urgent demand of the moment lies exactly in the differentiation and the outlining of the boundaries of what submits to your ego and what submits to the Divine Law inside of you. And the sooner you are able to understand this, the faster you will get rid of all that is not from God in you.

These processes of differentiation and recognizing are so subtle and so unyielding to the earthly logic that you will have to face serious life trials in the near future, which will finally make you think about the separation of the real from the unreal within you.

Beloved, all the external manifestations of disharmony — any weather anomalies and catastrophes — all happen thanks to the incongruity of your consciousness with the Will of God. There is a vector in accordance with which planet Earth was prescribed to evolve. And there are vectors of your aspirations. If the vectors of your aspirations do not coincide with the basic course of evolution prescribed for this planet, the vectors of your personal aspirations will be abruptly changed by the external forces.

If you meet with extremely great counteraction in the outer world around you, think about whether all your actions are performed in accordance with the Will of God.

However, there is a diametrically opposed tendency nowadays and it is strong enough. It is when your aspirations are completely in keeping with the Will of God and the vector of your aspirations is rightly directed, but you are surrounded by forces which do not wish to change and understand subconsciously and sometimes quite consciously that you represent a source of danger for them. You bring into this world the Divine Energy of change, the fresh wind of change.

Therefore, you will face resistance from the side of the forces which do not want any changes.

That is why I bring you back to the thought that it is necessary for you to make differentiations in your life constantly. Every minute and every second of your life on Earth you make a choice, changing not only your future but also the future of the whole planet.

When I offered you my sponsorship, I did it with the purpose of enabling everything that acts correspondingly with the direction of the vector of the Divine evolution. I will take all the measures available to me to protect you from the excessive resistance of the forces counteracting the general course of evolution.

But if you asked for my sponsorship, wishing to derive personal benefit and to find personal success and prosperity, I would also take you under my control, but my help in this case would just contribute to your facing such inner and outer circumstances in your life that would make you think about whether you really acted in harmony with the Will of God.

Perform only constant hard work and development but no rest, beloved. You have come to this world to act, and you will act whether you want to or not.

It is impossible to deceive God, beloved; it is impossible to deceive me. I read your hearts, and I see your real motives and true aspirations.

If you clash with insurmountable barriers in life, first of all you need to differentiate whether these barriers are the consequence of the wrong direction of movement chosen by you and the wrong vector of your aspirations, or whether these barriers are the result of the resistance of the dark forces hindering you exactly because your aspirations are entirely congruent to the Will of God.

And if the barriers in your life are caused by the resistance of the dark forces, you make an appeal and ask for my help — and the insurmountable barrier will be dissolved by the legions of the Light. This will happen as quickly as will be allowed by the outer circumstances and so naturally that you will forget in a while that this insurmountable barrier faced you not long ago.

Those of you wishing to derive a personal benefit from my sponsorship will have to think over their motives and reevaluate their consumer approach to the help of Heaven very soon.

Therefore, do not try, beloved, to make God play the game according to your rules. The rules of the game were established once and forever at the moment of creation of the material universe. In accordance with these rules, a cosmic moment has come now when you must give up any personal aspirations and everything inside of you which is not in harmony with the Will of God.

It is not an instantaneous process, of course, and this process will take much longer than the length of one of your earthly lives. But do always remember that the days of the chosen are shortened. If you wish to end the cycle of existence of your ego, and to finally part with it in this life, you will be rendered all the possible help of Heaven. But do not forget that in this case you choose the accelerated return of your karma, which can lead to serious complications in your life.

That is why this speeded Path is impossible for most of you, because your karma is so hard that it is physically impossible to organize the return of it during one lifetime because of the natural laws governing in the material world. I do not even say that your physical body simply will not bear such a forced return of the karma.

Today I have explained to you the criteria which I follow when giving you my help. And I have explained to you in detail what my help to you is in reality. First of all, I help your soul and the immortal part of you. I simply do not take into account your physical body and everything connected with a quiet and prosperous dwelling of your body in the physical world.

Your physical body must be in a working state, but only when you fulfil the Will of God and do not use your physical temple for receiving pleasures in this world.

Therefore, if someone meets no obstructions in his life and uses life only for pleasure, I would think about whether this person is alive and whether his inner person has left him to let him live out his days quietly. Does this person have a future? Maybe he is a dead man, living out his days in luxury thanks to the mercy of Heaven. After all, everybody receives according to their just rewards and aspirations.

My talk could have seemed stern and impartial to you today. Well, my task is not to give compliments and fuss over those of you who do not wish to follow the Will of God and the Law of this universe. For those of you who are ready to follow the Will of God, I will be a much more caring nurse than you would ever be able to find in the physical plane.

I AM El Morya Khan.

Aspiration, constancy and devotion — these are the qualities necessary for our disciples

May 14, 2005

I AM El Morya, having come to you through my messenger again.

I AM. And I AM just as real, if not more real, than everything that surrounds you in your illusory world. We provide our disciples with the training which first of all concerns the expansion of your consciousness and the recognition of our world which is beyond the limits of perception of your sensory organs; but it does not become less real because of that.

I have come to put into plain words the understanding of communication between the worlds and to ascertain it in your consciousness.

We are constantly beside you in your earthly toil and concerns, but we cannot divert you from your concerns unless you yourselves want to apply to us.

Believe that our world is constantly next to you. It is only the level of your vibrations that separates us from each other. Raise your vibrations and aspire to communicate with us, and you will receive what you seek.

The difficulty is in your ability to recognize by your external consciousness both our presence and the opportunity to contact us.

You ask for signs, and we give signs. You ask for help, and we give help. You ask for communication with us, and we enter into the communication with you. But why, when asking for all that, do you immediately forget what you ask for? When we come to your call, your consciousness appears to be so deep in your illusory world that you are not able to hear us.

That is why I have come to remind you about the constant discipline of your consciousness and mind which you must submit to if you really want to be our disciples. We do not need followers who say that they want to be our disciples, ask us for help, but whose consciousness happens to be so carried away by the illusion that surrounds them that they forget about all their applications, promises, oaths, and assurances after just a few hours.

We need disciples, but if you really want to receive training under the guidance of the Ascended Masters, please be kind enough to devote at least some feeble efforts to it.

Remember that you should not wish to be our disciples from time to time, when you occasionally think of us amidst your everyday bustle. No, you should constantly remember what you want to reach and what you aspire to. You should keep your consciousness directed to our world and aspired to our world, no matter what difficult life situations you get into.

Aspiration, constancy, and devotion — these are the qualities necessary for our disciples.

You may do your everyday routine and household chores, but you should always keep in mind the image of our world. You should keep the consonance with us all of the time.

This will enable you to develop perceptibility, sensibility to our needs and the requirements of the hour.

We keep a twenty-four hour watch on the planet and allow ourselves to have only a little rest plunging into nirvana for a short time.

What stops you from following our example? Keep and maintain your sensibility and focus during the day. So that when a need for your help arises or when the time comes for you to have your lesson, you don't miss that moment, because of being distracted by useless chatter, unnecessary arguments, or watching one more serial.

When you want to become our disciples and to receive our guidance, instructions, and help, why do you think that you are freed from the responsibilities you must share with us?

We can come and give you a lesson, a task, or information at any time of the day or night. That is why your responsibility is to be sensitive at all times if you enter the ranks of our disciples.

When you study at a school or university, your duty is to attend lectures and listen to your teachers. The teachers may put you in detention or even suspend you from school for negligence. Why do you consider training under our guidance to be less responsible?

When you receive knowledge in your educational institutions, you need this knowledge mostly in your current life. We give you the knowledge which you will need during all of your lives. So why do you let yourselves miss our trainings and shirk your duties?

The peculiarity of our training is that in the process of giving it to you, we do not divert you from your life duties. You may be at work and go through our training. You may be at home taking care of your child and go through training under our guidance.

Therefore, you should constantly stay aware and wait for our tasks, our instructions, and for the information coming from us.

We do not communicate with our disciples in their language. We send our knowledge and our information in a form of energy: a slight breath of wind, a little flash of light, a small arising wish, or emerging energy enabling you to perform some task. It is very seldom that we say something to our disciples. Our words occur in your minds as naturally as if they were your own thoughts. Only after a while, you can realize that these thoughts came to you from us.

Therefore, you should constantly be sensitive and be ready to receive our information and our instructions.

Do not expect me or one of the Masters to come to you in all magnitude and to talk to you, to give you teachings, and answer your questions. We do not have physical bodies; therefore, we hardly ever spend our power and energy in order to appear in front of our disciples in a densely astral form. If you want to be trained by us, you should refine your perceptibility to such an extent that will allow you to be sensitive to our words, our needs, and our requirements.

Develop your gift of making distinctions. Many astral dwellers can make fun of you and pretend to be the Masters. Many of them are far from being friendly, and many are simply very spiteful and vindictive.

Your own state of consciousness is the best criterion for you when you judge whom you are dealing with in the higher plane. You know that like draws to like. If you are not balanced and harmonious inside, if you harbor within you any negative feelings inherent in people, then you will hardly receive communication with the real Ascended Masters.

Therefore, pay attention to the level of your consciousness during the day. Your consciousness is very mobile. I may say that during the day you continually glide in your consciousness along some scale from its lowest to its highest level. Everything you encounter in life influences the level of your consciousness, including all the people whose auras come into contact with yours, films that you watch, and music that you listen to.

78

Literally everything in your world affects you. Thus, your main task is to maintain the level of your consciousness at the highest level available to you for the most part of the day.

Find time to retire from everyone for at least a few minutes every day, and analyze your state during the day — all of the thoughts, feelings, and images coming to you.

Constantly analyze your state and scrutinize your feelings over and over again.

We are beside you all of the time, and it is only the level of your vibrations and the level of your consciousness that prevents you from seeing and hearing us.

The first thing you should do is to learn to distinguish our presence and our vibrations.

Our best disciples never leave their watch. They constantly keep their consonance with us and are ready to receive the necessary instructions from us twenty-four hours a day.

Therefore, instead of feeling hurt by the Masters if they do not pay proper attention to you and do not give you the necessary help, scrutinize your inner state. Haven't you missed our lesson and our help because you have been too busy complaining about your hard life and paying too much attention to the illusion around you?

I have given my exhortation today in the hope that you will understand our difficulties occurring in the case when you ask for our help and we give you that help, but you simply do not notice it because you are too busy with your earthly problems.

I AM El Morya.

You must act, act and act

May 21, 2005

I AM El Morya, having come through my messenger.

Today special circumstances have forced me to give you a short epistle-exhortation. Accept it with all your attention and gravity.

The brevity of my words will make them more intelligible.

The haste creates the necessary tenseness.

The space is stressed. The currents are amplified.

The news from our world is well-timed.

Be on the *qui vive*. Prepare to act.

The general lull on earth is deceitful. Changes are approaching, and events are coming which will be remembered by their seemingly dramatic character and perpetuity.

However, let's get rid of the needless and obsolete. Let's take care of the new and progressive.

Those who are with us in their aspirations and service should not worry about anything. Those impudent in relation to the Divine plan and thinking of themselves as gods, will be put in their place.

There is no intention to intimidate you with this message. Everyone will receive according to his desserts, and everyone knows in their heart to what extent they act in accordance with the Higher Law.

There is boldness from the Light, when the servants direct all their strength and energy towards the Common Wealth and the Good.

There is dark impudence when an individual challenges the forces of Light and takes the absence of a prompt punishment to be the inability of the Light forces to react to his impudence.

Irrespective of the fact, whether these hostile carpers act within the framework of any religion or whether they prefer to do evil in the shadow of the powers that be, their time is up and soon they will have to be called to account.

Angels strictly record all the abusive words and all the brazen actions. There is always an opportunity to choose another path. There is always a chance to repent and to accept the retribution with humility.

Every time we say it and every time people do not believe that it relates to them. The human memory is short. And when the time comes to be called to account, they wonder, "Do we really owe so much?"

Therefore, think before you create debts. The time flows constantly and implacably. The gush of the Divine Energy is interminable. And there is no chance to stop time.

Therefore, think over the direction of your attention at every minute of your life. Your energy flows where your attention is directed. But if you stop for a moment and objectively scrutinize your thoughts during the day, you will be filled with horror. Ninety percent of your attention is drawn to the things which do not deserve even a glance.

The control over thoughts and feelings comes to the fore nowadays.

There is no prospect to postpone the retribution. The period for the return of the karma of your actions has been shortened. You will hardly have time to perform an act of evil before the retribution follows. And there will be no need to ask anybody: "What for, oh Lord?"

The severe conditions of the world force us to take tough and urgent response measures.

The period of infancy has come to an end. And you will no longer have a caring mommy to take the burden of your troubles upon her.

The period of maturity has come, and you will have to be responsible for every action, every thought, and for all that you admit in your consciousness that does not correspond to the Will of God.

It is necessary to free the space and the building site before laying the foundation for something new.

This is a matter of our concern now and we are making every effort to obtain this. We have purified the higher planes; now it is the turn of the lower ones.

A capital clearing up has been started on earth. Take care; do not let the Divine broom catch you on its way!

I am warning you, because much depends on you these days. Not only are your merits of importance now, but also the correlation of the mutual efforts of the two sides. There is no time left to wait for the karma to be transmuted. The peculiarity of the current period is in the rapid return of whatever you have made. You will hardly have time to start praying before a situation demanding your reaction crops up.

Remember, even if you react wrongly in an unexpected situation, you still pass through tests and work off your karma. You work off your karma and pass through tests exactly when you draw useful lessons from the situations that you get into in your life.

I watch all the people under my wardship who have asked for my sponsorship and protection. But this does not mean that I will protect them from problems and plights. Those whom God most loves, He most tests, because only after the conquering of the tribulations you do grow, you multiply your abilities, and expand your consciousness.

It is vital to give you the understanding of the barriers that you encounter and to remind you in good time about the importance of overcoming inflexibility, aspiration, and bravery.

There are no grumblers and idlers among my disciples.

I say, "Urgency! Hit the road!" And all my disciples are ready.

You can do up your dress on the move, and you can understand how to act better without halting.

Therefore, keep sensibility. I expect you to be prompt at my first call.

Do not expect me to come and to shout into your ears. Just look at my portrait and you will be aware of the urgent things to do.

There is no time left to waste on idle talk. The current situation requires actions.

That's why you should act, act and act. Try to use every minute of your life on earth.

Think this over. You have been waiting for an opportunity to start acting for thousands of years. The time is ripe for actions. It is high time to act.

For that reason, do not whine that you have not had enough time to get ready, that your boots are full of holes, and you have not packed all your things into a knapsack.

Leave all your things. You will need nothing but your wish to serve and the fire of your hearts.

Do not care about your tomorrow and the day after tomorrow.

Do not think of your yesterday and the day before yesterday.

This can disturb you on your path. Think of the things happening now and make every effort to serve best.

Do not force me to send a herald to you to remind you about your mission. All the knowledge and the entire plan are always with you in your hearts.

I say, "Quickly." I say, "Urgently." And you should carry out what you must. Today exactly the moment has come, for the sake of which you have come into embodiment. Everything has to be changed. A capital clearing up has been started on earth. Climb up to the attics of your consciousness. Descend into the cellars of your dark wishes. Take out your dirty laundry.

Everything is to be washed, cleaned, and dried.

There will be none of your old clothing left unclean and unwashed.

Do not be afraid to give up the old rags of your egoistic thoughts and feelings.

All this will burn in the flame of your service and in the fire of your hearts.

There is no place for imperfection in the new world.

I say, the dawn is nearing, and it is time to get up and start acting.

The new time is coming! Do meet it!

I AM El Morya, and I have addressed my devoted disciples.

Kindle your torches and set off to bestow your flame to the world

May 25, 2005

I AM El Morya, having come to you through my messenger.

Our meeting today will be fully devoted to our actions connected with Russia and the problems which we have to solve in this country in order to implement our plans.

You know that during the last hundred and fifty years we have been trying to go ahead with our plans concerning this country which stands aloof from many countries and cannot be compared with any of them. But every time we set out to implement our plans and found a person-transmitter in the physical plane through which we could act, the opposing forces turned against us, and we had to go back on a decision.

However, no one can escape his destiny. Since there is a plan from God for this country, Russia — and

I assure you that such a plan does exist — it must be put into action. All the difficulties can just harden a warrior on the Path. The obstacles are needed exactly to help warriors to acquire experience and better skills.

If you, your parents, and your grandfathers had not overcome the severe tests that had befallen them during the last century, you would scarcely be able to comprehend our Teaching now.

It is a delusion to think that we sustained a defeat. This defeat, beloved, is related only to the physical plane. All the sacrifices that were made in this country during the years of wars, revolutions, and repressions were made only in the physical plane. But if you look at the events happening in the higher plane at that time, you will see a gigantic evolution of souls. You will see the opportunities that were provided to each soul for its development.

You can see that some people sacrificed for the sake of Common Wealth and the Good, while others committed dreadful crimes and created karma pursuing the transient benefit in the physical plane.

That is how it happened during the entire period of modern history.

God wants you to evolve. God wants you to perfect yourselves and to develop.

For as long as God has loved Russia and its inhabitants, He has been giving the people of this country a chance to go through accelerated tests and accelerated development.

A lot has been endured; a lot of grief and suffering had to be felt keenly. Today the country is in a deep spiritual crisis and is enduring the years of a deep stagnation.

This is the result of the karma of atheism that was permitted by the people. Just imagine that right now a new generation of people is being born who in their previous lives fought with each other in the fields of the civil war and met each other at the interrogations during the repressions.

You can picture the former victims and executioners right now sitting at one desk at school — those who killed and those who were executed and tormented. But the karma has not disappeared. The karma remains, and the karma must be worked out.

You know that if a pendulum has deviated to one side, then according to the law of physics it inevitably has to deviate to the other side with the same amplitude. If during the last hundred years you have been watching the deviation of the pendulum towards the side of atheism, distrust, and rejection of the Supreme Law for everything which exists, this means, beloved, that Russia is predestined to have Faith in God and to have Faith in the Supreme Law during the next hundred years. As long as these hundred years have not passed without leaving a trace in the evolution of people's souls, the experience acquired by these souls will no longer allow them to be carried away by the blind faith and dogmas of any external church.

That is why we are beginning the new cycle in a state of a full spiritual vacuum, and it makes it even easier for us to plant the verdure of the new knowledge, new ideas, and new understanding of the structure of the world in the hearts and minds of the generation living in Russia today.

Neither the collapse in the physical plane, nor the irreparability in the minds of people can be barriers. The most important thing is to sow the seeds of aspiration within people's minds and hearts, to kindle the fire of knowledge, and to fan the flames of the Divine Freedom.

You have gotten used to relying on the external. You have gotten used to making plans that are based on the external knowledge received by your mind. The time has come when you must give God an opportunity to act through you. All you need for that, beloved, is to get rid of your ego and of all your attachments to the things of this world. You should provide your temples for the Divine guidance. Your ego obstructs us, as well as the bustle of your minds and your empty inquisitiveness.

You should simply pin your hopes upon the Will of God. You must fully submit to the Will of God.

The Will of God is not manifested in the churches. There is no organization in the physical plane that acts in accordance with the Will of God. The Will of God, beloved, can be manifested only through you, through your hearts. That is why you should long to provide all your lower bodies for the realization of the Will of God for this country.

You should be possessed by the realization of the Will of God. You should be possessed by the aspiration to become an obedient tool of God in the process of implementing the plan for this country.

I do not ask you to submit your will to any external organization. I do not ask you to apply for any instructions to the messenger through whom I am giving this dictation.

No, beloved. You do not need a mediator between you and God, between you and the Ascended Hosts any longer.

Your Higher Self and your Guardian Angel are always aware of the Divine plan for your lifestream. You do not need to go to messengers, clairvoyants, psychics, or servants of the cults in order to know the plan of God for your lifestream. Everything is written in your heart.

Tell me, how many of you have talked to your heart lately? How many of you have tried to understand what your heart tells you?

You are so busy in your life that it is hard for you to find at least five minutes to be alone with yourself in silence, far from the vanity.

Your heart is constantly trying to talk to you. But you do not hear it. You prefer to listen to your friends and acquaintances, to watch TV, to listen to your horrible music, or to pick up knowledge from newspapers, books, and magazines.

Beloved, there is no source of information in your world that can tell you what your life plan is, why you have been embodied, and what you are to do now and in the near future.

You will not hear about it on the radio, you will not manage to learn about it from the TV programs. You cannot read about this in any books.

Your heart is keeping the innermost information, so necessary for you, and it longs to share this information with you.

All the Ascended Hosts, beloved, are ready to give you all the possible ministration in your Divine task for the sake of which you have come into embodiment on planet Earth at this difficult time.

Why do you ignore the help of Heaven?

How long will you scour your beggarly world in search of the sense of life? You will never find the sense of life in the surrounding world! I tell you this with a full sense of responsibility, because it is impossible for the mortal to inherit the immortal. The essence of your nature is Divine. And you must return to your Divine nature.

Your search for the sense of life in the physical plane is doomed to failure from the very start. The only true Path lies within you, inside of your hearts. There are many paths in this world that people prefer to follow from one embodiment to another, from life to life. But the only true Path is discarded by them.

God is patient, beloved. No matter how long you wander around the external world, the time will come when you will return Home.

Therefore, your major task for the present time is to feel this Path in your heart. And you will become living guides on this Path for many lost souls.

When you start following the Path leading you Home, you will have to give up the superfluous burden that makes you encumbered and attached to the physical world.

Your vibrations will rise, your thoughts and feelings will become purified, and you will serve as a luminary on the Path for those who are still continuing to wander in the dark.

All the miracles and treasures of the world are hidden in the depth of your hearts. When you manage to kindle a torch in your heart, everything will change within you and around you.

We need devoted collaborators. We need warriors of Light whom we can count on in the implementation of our plans for this country and for the entire humanity.

Kindle your torches and set off to bestow your flame to the world.

I AM El Morya, and I am giving you the flame of knowledge.

Russia is spring cleaning now

June 9, 2005

I AM El Morya, having come again.

To tell you that it is vital to give these dictations and it is important that you read them is telling you nothing. Each time, we make every effort to overcome the resistance of the matter and the resistance of the circumstances related to the transmission of our messages to the physical octave. The difficulty is in bringing the transmission of the messages into harmony with the tasks of the present day as much as possible. The top of the agenda of the day is to transform the consciousness of earthlings, to raise the level of their consciousness, and to expand its capacity. Your consciousness is the only barrier getting in the way of your communication with us, and your consciousness is the main barrier preventing the situation on planet Earth from changing. That is why I keep coming to you and saying over and over again: "Strain every nerve. Get rid of everything unnecessary that is stagnating in your consciousness and which should not take place in the New World."

The development of Russia seems to have come to a dead end. It seems that nothing is changing and everything is bad. But do not judge by the external manifestations because inside of every human, inside of every light-bearer who is in embodiment and lives in the territory of Russia, great progress in the transformation of their consciousness is taking place now. Arduous work is being done on the re-evaluation of the experiences of the last hundred years. There is a proverb: "A negative result is still a result." This proverb excellently matches the events which Russia lived through during the last century. It is impossible, beloved, to build up a new society compliant with the standards of the New World if you do not base it on the Faith in God — the true Faith, but not the faith which was forcibly swept away in the course of the Revolution in 1917. The Russian people have always intuitively understood that no official religion with its hierarchy and its wish to obtrude its dogmas can cope with the spiritual needs of the generous Russian spirit. It should be understood that the capacity of the consciousness of a Russian man has expanded considerably during the last decades. Sometimes external explosions and social disruptions have to take place in order to help to get rid of the hindering dogma and to conquer it within consciousness. This process is akin to a process of spring cleaning in your house. At first sight it may seem to you that you are surrounded by complete disorder and chaos. All the things that used to be in their proper places have been displaced and it is impossible to find them. Other things have become dilapidated and must be replaced, so you throw them away. Of course, you are sorry to part with your favorite things that were serving you hand and foot during many years and that literally became part and parcel of you. But the time comes for you to rummage through your wardrobe and take out the old things and junk them. You dust and polish the things that can still serve you and put them in their proper places again.

Russia is having a bout of cleaning now. A grandiose rethinking of the values is taking place. Moreover, all the people of Russia are taking part in this spring cleaning. That is why the country looks so rough — hence the frowning faces. The bout of cleaning is going full blast. And it seems that there is no end to this tiring work. Many people are trying to return to the articles of belief of their great-grandfathers. They return to the newly restored temples, listen to their heart and reason, smell the aromas of the church odors. And it bodes well that the future of Russia is connected precisely with God and the true Faith in God. Yet, a soul cannot find sanctuary in the old faith. Literally crowds of people are busy seeking new movements and new religions. And the forces of darkness happily throw the surrogates of the faith to you, beautiful things that are, however, absolutely useless for the evolution of the soul. The people of the great country are choosing which to decide in favor of, which to prefer, and which to give up. But maybe it is useful to preserve something, to rub away the layer of dust from it and to shelve it? Just the same thing relates to the social life. After many years of domination of the false community, some people try to return to this community, but to rebuild it on new principles. Others called to mind even older times and are trying to entrench themselves among the new elite, wishing to introduce into the country the same inequality that was characteristic of the last years of the Tsar's regime. And it seems again that something is going wrong. There is a proverbial wisdom saying that one cannot step into the same water twice. But it is too painful to part with the old things, to throw them away. Yet the sooner the collective consciousness of people gets rid of the old unneeded dogmas — both in the clerical and in the secular life — the sooner and more successfully will the new take an independent stand in the consciousness of people.

We are happy to watch the sprouts of the new and progressive in the hearts and minds of many people. Our disciples know neither sleep nor rest. Our true disciples are working around the clock. Our guards are keeping watch day and night. The natal stronghold must be protected from what is uncongenial to the New World, from any ideas that come from the civilized world of Europe and America. Yet, I must say that there is nothing behind the entire so-called western civilization that might be needed in the future society. No matter how strange it may seem to you, I will tell you that both Europe and America have irrecoverably fallen far behind the people of Russia when judged by the level of their spiritual development and the level of their consciousness. You do not see it now, when you are amid the chaos of your current spring cleaning. Believe me; literally, in a few years the changes in the consciousness that are in progress now by leaps and bounds, and the path and pace of which are just without parallel, will be manifested in the surrounding life. Everything around you is the reflection of your consciousness. The picture that you watch around you now is the reflection of the consciousness that the Russian society had during the period of the false community — so-called socialism.

The matter is the most inert part of the universe. It takes years for the changes in the consciousness to be manifested in the physical world. Before now, it took much more time to reflect the transformation of consciousness than it does at present. But the time has changed. Any changes in the consciousness of people lead to almost instantaneous changes in the physical plane. Their momentariness is measured in the cosmic scale, indeed. Nevertheless, the process of acceleration, the process of the raising of the vibrations of the world is in progress constantly and inevitably. That is why the time allowed for the transformation of consciousness to be manifested in the physical plane is shortened every year. Therefore, do aspire to transform your consciousness. Bring discipline to your consciousness. You have your past before you as an example — your faith that was repudiated, and you see the shots taken at its restoration. But this faith cannot satisfy people any longer because their consciousness has expanded, and it cannot be squeezed within the old framework. The former false community exists no more, since the true community can be based only on the true Faith. The old system, when a few possessed everything and masses of people were close to starving, cannot be reestablished because it does not answer the purposes of the present time. The combination of the true community is based on the true Faith; the social structure of the society takes care and renders help to all its members, especially paying attention to the children and the disabled. Each member of the society has the opportunity to develop freely, to receive free education and the best medical assistance. All of these things, which existed in the false community, should be re-railed nowadays according to the true Faith, and they will mold the image of the future structure of the New Age that we keep in our hearts.

The social inequality and the inequalities in wealth will be overcome after the renovation of the system of education. This new system will give the future generation the knowledge about the Divine Laws governing in this universe and about the main laws — the law of karma, or retribution, and the law of reincarnation or evolution of the souls.

All of the fundamentals of the true Faith must be brought back to the society. Every person must gain understanding of the change of the cycles and of the necessity to get rid of his ego and to perfect himself in God.

We are giving the guidelines. We are giving the basics. We are giving the instructions. For those who can hear. For those who can acknowledge. For those who are ready.

I AM El Morya.

A Teaching on Freedom[23]

June 19, 2005

I AM El Morya, having come again!

I hope that our meeting today will be of benefit for you in your knowing of the world. During many years we have been trying to develop in our messenger an ability not only to perceive the knowledge she already had within her consciousness to one extent or another, but also to be able to pass on the torch that was absolutely new for her. As a result, our every attempt enabled us to stock your mind more and more with knowledge and comprehension.

---

[23] During the message transmission a computer fault occurred. The receiving of the dictations is performed by me with the simultaneous recording of the incoming information on the computer. I have only managed to restore the beginning of the received dictation. The major part of the typed text had been destroyed. While I was trying to recover the lost text, I fell out of the information flow and was unable to continue receiving. Therefore, I publish that part which I managed to save. Going forward we'll see if the computer and the external conditions will allow me to continue receiving the messages. (Tatyana Mickushina)

You know that the universe is organized so that each level of the universe with its own level of consciousness is separated from the previous and the next levels by a kind of impenetrable energetic barrier. You obtain an ability to overcome these barriers only when you acquire a certain inner energetic potential that enables you to do that. The energy that you are able to assimilate is determined by the level of the development of your consciousness. The more developed your consciousness is, the higher energetic layers you can get access to. For that reason, the level of your vibrations endows you with a certain level of freedom.

In fact, the whole evolution consists in the process of your attainment of a larger level of freedom, which will enable you to assimilate by your consciousness a large number of energetic layers and to get access to an enormous amount of information.

The paradox lies in the fact that you should first give up your free will in the way you view it at your human level of consciousness. Freedom is understood by a human as a lack of restrictions for the satisfaction of his wishes. If the laws of your society do not restrict by enforcement the freedom of individual members of the society, then the ungovernable lusts of some of them will be able to harm the entire human population existing on the planet.

First, you must willingly give up in your consciousness, your carnal mind, and the human wishes and needs connected with it. After doing that you will obtain a larger degree of freedom providing you with access to the higher energetic and informational levels…

Your consciousness is the only restriction of your Divine Freedom

June 21, 2005

I AM El Morya, having come to you again.

The situation that occurred during the receiving of my last dictation[24] reminded me about the fact that the opposing forces maintain their combat readiness, and they will not be slow to take advantage of any gap in our defense.

Three detachments of angels, 144 angels in each, secure the receiving of each dictation.

In addition, Archangel Michael's legions of angels of defense are heavily involved. But, in spite of this seemingly impenetrable wall, the forces of the dark manage to defeat us at the most inappropriate moment.

---

[24] While receiving the dictation of El Morya from June 19, 2005, the major part of the dictation was lost because of a computer fault.

Well, this world represents a battlefield between two opposing forces. And until the feeling of conflict is blotted out of the consciousness of the last embodied individual, the conflict will go on.

Picture two armies ready for a battle. The files of the warriors are deployed in battle order. Their faces are stiff. Every warrior is only waiting for a command to join battle.

Your position in the world is like that of those warriors.

And now imagine that a miracle takes place. A sunburst appears through the sinister clouds hanging over the battlefield, and it spotlights both the battlefield and the severe frowning faces of the warriors. Can you imagine at least for a moment that a miracle can happen and the soft sun-rays penetrating the clouds can dissolve any hostile feelings in the hearts of the warriors?

Can you imagine that the inner state of the warriors can be transformed? One thought, one impulse from the heart of every warrior is enough to endow the consciousness and the external mind of every combatant with a more elevated character.

When you are able to rise onto a higher level in your consciousness, you can notice that everything separating you from your enemies and rivals before loses its significance. It is because you are struck by the beauty and the omnipotence of the Divine Truth suddenly bursting upon your view. And you are not able to feel any hostile feelings any more as you experience your unity with every particle of life. And you feel the pain of every particle of life. You realize that any feeling of conflict, any feelings of hatred or dislike are not Divine and that the people that have come under the influence of such negative feelings are just to be pitied. And you understand that you can help these people. You can endue them with your feeling of Love and your understanding and give them a particle of the Divine Energy that will enable your rivals to feel your Love.

Just as the Sun bursting through the clouds is capable of sending you a ray of hope and endowing you with a feeling of love and compassion at times, you can endue every person that you meet in your life with the Love from your heart.

Believe me, it is only Love that is able to oust all the negative manifestations from your world.

However, I would like to return to the topic of our interrupted conversation: to the quality of Freedom, Divine Freedom, and to the understanding of this quality by the Ascended Hosts.

The understanding of Freedom as total permissiveness and the absence of any restrictions is a distortion of the quality of the Divine Freedom inherent in the Ascended Hosts.

In exactly the same way as you in your world restrict all the manifestations of insatiable lusts and aspirations of separate individuals capable of harming other people, there is a restriction in the Divine world.

The energetic barrier that exists between our worlds cannot admit to our world the individuals who have not subdued their consciousness to the Law governing in this universe.

Any imperfect manifestations, including the imperfect quality of freedom which is present in the minds of the mortals, cannot penetrate the energetic barrier separating us. In order for you to be able to overcome this barrier, you must successively give up all of the non-divine qualities and manifestations in your being and substitute them with perfect models and manifestations.

As you perform this difficult work upon yourselves, you free yourselves from the negative energies contained in your aura. Your auras become attuned with the Divine reality, your chakras open, and the level of your vibrations allows you, first, to dwell in our world — in the etheric octaves — for a short time and next, when you confirm your achievements and corroborate the achieved level by passing numerous tests, you acquire the right to be present among the Ascended Hosts and become one of us.

In exchange for rejecting your imperfect qualities and your human understanding of freedom, you acquire the Divine Freedom — not as permissiveness but as the voluntary subordination of your entire being to the perfect Law governing in this universe. Only then, you receive the stage of freedom that enables you to overcome the barriers between the worlds and to get access to any information. You will be able to attend our libraries and to read the Akashi records. You will get access to any information that your consciousness is able to take in.

That is why your consciousness is the only restriction of your freedom, your Divine Freedom.

If the level of your consciousness is not high, but your desire for the journeys to other worlds is great, you can leave your body in your astral body and travel around the astral worlds. But you should never forget that your level of consciousness is your limiter and you will make journeys around those worlds that have the same level of vibrations as yours.

Therefore, we say that the worlds are open to you, but your main task is still to take care of your consciousness and its level and to aspire to get rid of any imperfection preventing your development.

You develop with your consciousness into the new worlds. You progress into different levels of the Heaven. And you surge higher and higher to the infinitude.

However, while you are in your material manifested world, you should never forget that in this sphere of your activity, as in any other one, some distortions are possible. You can master the technique of coming out of your body by training or by remembering the experience of your previous lives. But if you have not yet achieved a certain grade of purity of your four lower bodies, your journeys will take place within those levels of the astral and mental planes which are close to you by vibrations. And you will be unable to benefit from these journeys for the unfoldment of your soul. These exercises of yours will be similar to the journeys of drug addicts who, with the help of different chemical substances, reach a state in which their higher bodies separate from the physical body and make journeys around the astral plane.

As the worlds draw nearer, more and more people appear to be capable of receiving the abilities to communicate with the beings of the higher worlds.

You will need all your ability of making distinctions in order to form an opinion on the descriptions of the stories and experiences of the journeys to other worlds.

You should always remember that like draws to like. For that reason, keep an eye on a person who tells you about his experiences and experiments, trace his actions and opinions, and you will understand which worlds this person can visit.

There is nothing unusual in the fact that people can travel around the astral and the mental planes. You do it every night. But the point is in how much these journeys contribute to the evolution of your consciousness and how much they contribute to your progress on the Path.

Only perfecting yourselves in God is of importance. And your attachments to the astral and even to the mental planes must be overcome with time, as well as your attachments to the physical plane, because the lower levels of the higher plane cannot give your soul the knowledge it needs. You can wander around the valley for a long time, but we call you to the peak — to the summit of the Divine consciousness.

I am happy with the fact that our talk has taken place today.

I AM El Morya, and goodbye for the moment!

I congratulate you on the successful completion of this unique experiment on the transferring of the vital and timely information to the physical plane

June 30, 2005

I AM El Morya Khan, having come to you through this messenger today.

The events are unfolding at such a quick pace that the efforts of literally every light-bearer embodied now are of great importance. I am not sure if you are experiencing the changes that are taking place now with increasing strength and acceleration. In truth, the time for very quick and united actions has come. And those people who do not feel and understand this deserve only compassion because they have dropped out of the time and are trying to live according to the old precepts and to apply that yardstick to everything.

The New Age has come, and you have to attune your consciousness to it literally on your feet, because the rhythm of your life in the near future will require all your efforts, all your aspiration and all the fire of your hearts.

Therefore, even if nothing seems to have changed and everything is the same around you, do not believe your eyes. Everything is different! Everything around you has changed so decisively and irrevocably that no fantasy of yours will be enough to picture the transformations which are to come and which are already coming, though you cannot see them with your physical eyes. We have begun our steps forward. And we ask everybody who has been awakened, who feels the importance of the coming age and who is ready to dedicate his life to service, to get prepared. Very soon you, each of you in your town and country, will feel the changes that have begun.

It is difficult for you to believe in it, because everything around you seems to be the same as it was before. But I assure you that the most important transformation which we have been striving for during the last century and a half has taken place! Enough people who are in embodiment now have succeeded in the transformation of their consciousness, and this has yielded tangible results and manifestations in the physical plane. The period of time necessary for the transformation of consciousness to be materialized in the physical plane of planet Earth has also decreased. There were times when the change of consciousness was being materialized in the physical plane during tens and thousands of years.

At present, when your consciousness changes, it does not even take a night to start affecting your deeds.

I am trying to simplify my words in order to help you get an insight into the forthcoming time and opportunity.

Very soon you will be able to see in your life the consequences that will be caused by your transformed consciousness. If you do not see any changes in your life, this can be explained only by one thing — you have been flogging a dead horse while reading these dictations, because you have missed the main thing for the sake of which they have been given. You have failed to transform your consciousness. You have lost precious time and missed the invaluable opportunity granted to you by God.

As before, you thought you would be reading nice words in these dictations and that was all you needed. You were mistaken, since in addition to the reading of the nice words, you were required to undertake concrete actions that with a 100% probability should have brought you to a result — to the transformation of your consciousness, if you only had not been lazy and had read these dictations not as mere simple words, but as a guidance for practical actions in the physical plane.

Well, those of you who have missed this chance to pass through the accelerated course of initiations and transformation of your consciousness will receive an opportunity to repeat a class and to reread all the dictations given through this messenger beginning with the very first one from the 4th of March of this year.

And if you still do not feel any transformation of your consciousness and do not see any changes in your life, I recommend that you reread these dictations a third time.

You have received an invaluable and a completely unique gift in the form of these dictations. You cannot even imagine how much energy has been spent by the Ascended Hosts in order to transmit these dictations through the Internet right to your homes and how many angels have been involved! I am not speaking now about the efforts made by Tatyana while receiving these dictations. You cannot even realize what it was for her to withstand such a flow of information and energy daily and to be able to maintain herself in a good shape during almost four months without missing a day.

At the beginning of this experiment none of us was sure that we would be able to perform the transmission of such important information in such volume and within such a short period of time. But now we can bravely state that our experiment has succeeded! The work has been fulfilled and fulfilled perfectly!

I congratulate you, and I congratulate Tatyana on the successful completion of this unique experiment on the transferring of the vital and timely information to the physical plane. The work is to be continued, but its major stage is over — the informational stage — when the physical plane of the planet received the information which is so necessary exactly for the current moment. You will still have an opportunity to receive all the necessary explanations. And we will continue our work through our messenger Tatyana.

The new stage is coming — the stage when the information given by us in the dictations will develop in the hearts of people. Everybody will be able to find an outlet for his energy and an application for his abilities.

There is enough work for everybody! The important work upon the transformation of the physical plane is just beginning. And everyone who has managed to awaken his consciousness and to kindle the fire in his heart will become a source of knowledge, information, and energy for everybody whom he meets in his life. Your task as the light-bearers is to constantly maintain the flame of your torches and to bring the Light to the world.

All of you who have managed to awaken your consciousness while reading these dictations will receive from me a thin thread which will connect you with me and support you in the trying moments.

All you need is just to make a call:

"**In the name of I AM THAT I AM, I invoke the action of the thread connecting me with Master El Morya. Master El Morya, please help me in my situation** (describe the situation in detail). **Help me to find a Divine solution for my situation and give me the help which the Supreme Law permits you to give.**"

And after you have made this appeal, I will help all of you who have deserved this personal connection with me due to your toil. You will certainly feel this thread connecting your hearts with mine. A lot of you feel this relationship by now.

I AM El Morya. I affirm that everything is possible when you are together with God!

Faith is the remedy that you need

December, 21, 2005

I have come to bring to your attention an important offer, which I am empowered to make this afternoon.

Just as during the previous cycle of dictations, I am now very determined. And if anyone of you doubts my determination and seriousness of my intentions, you'd better not read our messages, because you create in your consciousness an impassable barrier and block not only the stream of the Divine Truth, but the stream of the Divine Energy as well.

Your consciousness belongs to your dual world, therefore only those things happen in your world that you allow in your consciousness. That is why we will never fully tell you what kind of catastrophe you are probably facing, irrespective of the complexity of the situation on the planet. That is because if you only conceive the idea of a forthcoming catastrophe in your consciousness, this idea will be multiplied, and instead of extinguishing the existing fire you will be putting more and more wood into it.

That is why we will never fully tell you the information that we possess. But we will never cease to warn you and ask you to do all you can in order to harmonize the situation on the planet.

…the situation is actually tense. And no matter how hard we try, we have not yet been able to encourage you to assume those responsibilities that we are asking you about. The law of free will, which is operating in your physical octave, does not allow us to intervene and force you. That is why we can only ask you or, as a last resort, require of you. But it seems that the only thing that will make you take actions is the threatening circumstance that we are talking about.

Well, you seem to prefer acting in accordance with the Russian proverb, "One believes in wonder when hearing a sound of thunder."

There are very few people who seriously perceive our information and are ready to sacrifice much in order to comply with our requests.

We have not yet been able to enlarge the circle of people capable of specific actions. However, think about the fact that no matter how widely and promptly we give our warnings you are still unable to answer our call.

The problem is not even in your laziness and neglect. The whole point is that you are so captured by the illusion that you can differentiate neither what source contains the Truth nor the vibrations inherent to the true source.

Therefore, all your practices and all your actions should be directed at learning to make a distinction. In reality, staying in the illusion will come to an end only when you learn to make a distinction between the events that take place on the illusive plane and the events that belong to the real Divine world. Your task is to acquire a distinct vision and learn to give an evaluation to every event and fact that you face in life.

It seems to you that your life is running smoothly, and at times you don't even have an idea that in this silence and smooth flow of life there are hidden pitfalls, which are capable of turning the peaceful flow of your life upside down in a moment. Therefore, try to resist this soothing calmness. You are constantly getting your lessons. Sometimes one small stone lying on the rails is enough to make the huge train of your life derail at a great speed and turn over. However, you yourselves prepare your own future by making your everyday choices.

When the critical mass of your wrong choices reaches the limits of permissible karma, you encounter those situations in your life which literally destroy everything you are used to, and you exclaim in surprise, "Oh, Lord, what have I done? Why has it all fallen to my lot?"

It is a familiar picture, isn't it? At the next step, ninety percent of people start cursing God and the Masters for what has happened in their lives. They blame all the people around them and the whole world instead of humbly accepting all that has happened as a punishment or as a karmic retribution which overflowed the edges of the permissible limits and spilled in the form of a horrible punishment.

Thus, on one hand, in the course of the entire history of its existence, mankind has been guided and warned. On the other hand, only when something terrible happened to people were they able to think even if for a short time about the reasons things fell upon them.

And no matter how much we speak and give you the optimal advice in order to avoid the expected, you are not able to believe that everything you are told is true. The reason for your disobedience and shortsightedness is the lack of the true Faith.

That is why I, the Master who represents the aspect of God's Will, am addressing you this afternoon. I can help each of you who will turn to me with a request to strengthen their Faith.

Faith is the remedy that you need. I am speaking now not about blind faith based on ignorance and intimidation. I am referring to the Faith based on the exact knowledge of the Law that exists in this Universe.

This Law is the Law of cause and effect relationship, or the Law of Karma, or retribution. This Law operates regardless of your wish or your will. This is what is real. And that is what your aspiration to assert your free will, regardless of any circumstances, stumbles upon. If this natural barrier provided by the Creator did not stand in the path of misuse of your free will, the question of existence of not only your planet but the Universe itself would be put into challenge.

That is why the first thing that you should accept within yourselves is the supremacy of the Law governing in this Universe and in your lives.

You may appeal to me with the request to strengthen your Faith. I will gladly provide you with this aid as it is the most important and immediate remedy that you need.

I AM El Morya Khan, with faith in your victory!

Instructions about your attitude to everything around you in your dense world and in the finer worlds

April 20, 2006

I AM El Morya Khan, having come to you again through my messenger.

As it has been before, I have come to talk to you and to give instructions concerning your life and your place in the universe.

Like children who come to this world to explore it, you start the process of exploration of the world, but only of that world, which is still beyond the perception of your physical sense organs.

But that world exists; and it represents the Higher Reality in which you will be born and where you will stay in the course of time.

When your soul was in the fine world, before your incarnation, you were getting education and instructions about what you would face in the dense physical world. Now I come to give you directions about what you will face after your transition to the finer world.

The more you are ready for the transition to the finer world, the less effort your soul will have to apply to adapt to our world. We speak for everybody, but not everyone is able to perceive the information contained in the dictations and, especially, to read the information between the lines. That is the difference between the dictations that come from the Higher octaves and those messages that you get from the lower levels of astral and mental planes. The Messages are multidimensional.

The information is supposed to be understandable for everyone, regardless of their level of consciousness. However, there is something that is hidden behind the general phrases, and it only becomes understandable for those who can read between the lines and hear the voice in the silence of the quiet.

There is information for everyone, but not all can comprise everything.

Do not be confused with the fact that many things slip from your outer consciousness. There will be the time on your Path when you will suddenly start realizing what you have not been able to realize before. Knowledge will be coming into your head; and you will not understand why you know that. You will try to remember the source of the information but you won't be able to remember it. However, once you remember that you have been reading the Ascended Masters' dictations, you will realize that you have gotten the information between the lines unconsciously.

You join the certain information and energy egregore through reading these dictations, and you become able to come out to different layers of the finer world spontaneously and to get information from the Higher octaves directly. You get your education during your sleep, and you get your education in the form of insights and understanding, coming out to a high etheric level spontaneously.

Therefore, it is not as simple as it seems at first sight.

However, I have to prevent your anxiety. There will not be any information or any connection to the source of information without your consent. You can read these messages, feeling distrust of the source, feeling doubt, and with that you put an insurmountable energy barrier between you and us.

Only if your soul feels joy and triumph when reading our messages, and you express your willingness to get further education and further perception of the information, knowledge, and energy with all your being, only in this case Heavens open the opportunities before you, and you get access to our libraries, our classes, and databases.

It is similar to getting a password to access certain information. That password is given to you only when you express your willingness to cooperate with us and to get our information. However, on our side we evaluate the level of your consciousness, and you get access to those energies and information that you can assimilate. We watch carefully that the dose of energy received by you doesn't exceed the threshold which can be harmful for your health and subtle bodies.

Therefore, the process of penetration of the worlds and the process of cooperation of the worlds is under thorough control. A person with mercenary motives cannot get access to the information that he can use to cause harm to anybody. The criterion is always your vibrations. Each of you bears a unique vibration spectrum. You are a unique manifestation of the Divine Flame. The degree of your achievements puts non-washable traces on your Flame and your vibrations. So we can always distinguish you according to your flames and vibrations and, consequently, according to your consciousness level.

You should not worry that you do not get information directly from us. The process of transmission and accessing information from the higher plane is a century-old and tuned process. You get as much as you need and only when a suitable moment comes for that.

However, you should always be in a state of constant expectation. If you do not aspire or show your willingness, the energy will not be able to penetrate your aura, and you isolate yourself from the information that comes from the higher plane.

On the one hand, you should not worry that you do not get information; on the other hand, you should express constant willingness to receive the information right at the moment when it should come to you.

The combination of these two qualities which only seem incompatible becomes the barest necessity.

You get information when you are free of merely selfish desires to possess anything. The information arrives to you according to the extent you can get rid of the unreal part of you and, consequently, raise your vibrations to the level at which you can reach the octaves where that information becomes accessible for you.

There cannot be any standard approach for everybody. Everyone has a unique manifestation of Divinity in the physical world. And the main quality will be your ability to feel Love to Creator's plan and to never stop admiring all that diversity of Divine manifestations around you, not to focus on you and your problems but to watch the variety and diversity of Divine manifestations, to be able to see Divine miracles and enjoy them. That is why it is said that until you become like children, you will not be able to enter the Kingdom of Heaven.

Today I have given you some instructions about your attitude to your relations with each other and to the Divine Reality, and about your attitude to everything around you in your dense world and in the higher worlds.

I hope that the instructions received by you will help your development and enrich you.

<...>

I AM El Morya Khan, and I worship the Light of God within you.

We are calling you to follow our Path

April 30, 2006

I AM El Morya, coming to you!

...the time has come to accustom you to the Path that has been planned for you. This Path has always existed; and there were always Schools and Ashrams created in this or that part of the Earth where the Hierarchy of Light gave the Teaching for its disciples. The time has come when we see the possibility to resume our practice of working with non-ascended mankind through our outer Schools.

Therefore, we try to give all the necessary knowledge about The Path of Initiations, so you can consciously make your choice and step on the Path.

The difference between our Path and many other teachings is that we lead you through your heart and let you come into contact with the true Real world through your mystical experiences and insights. Having that possibility in your outer consciousness, to realize the existence of the other Divine world, you consciously aspire to become free of everything impeding you to enter that world. It is your ego and your attachments to the physical world, to things of this world and to people, as well as your habits and imperfections that impede you. Therefore, you consciously step on the Path and you are ready to sacrifice much in order to get the true knowledge. There are many other teachings that use very similar methods. Yet, there are some differences. Therefore, your immediate task is to find these differences, using the most reliable guide — your heart.

We are giving our Teaching through our messenger. Every one of you who reads our messages, already gets into the outer circle of our disciples and enters the Guru-Chela relationship with our messenger as a representative of our Hierarchy on the physical plane.

Therefore, as soon as you choose to read our messages, you already become our disciples. However, there are many levels of Guru-chela relationships. You mount the next step when you consciously make your choice in favor of our Teaching. In your consciousness you try to understand the difference from other teachings, and you make your choice in favor of the Teaching that you receive through our messenger. In this case you limit your freedom, yet, in return you acquire better understanding and better awareness of the knowledge that you receive through our messenger.

At the next level you consciously accept our messenger as your Guru. In this cycle of the dictations we hurried those of you, who are ready, to make this choice consciously and to rise to that level of your apprenticeship.

The next level begins when the messenger takes you as candidates for apprenticeship. The difference of that level from the previous ones is that the messenger partly takes on the karmic obligations and bears responsibility for her disciples. Further relations that you experience are entirely under the authority of our messenger. She determines how those relations should develop.

Therefore, we are trying to restore the Guru-chela relations which belong to the Ascended Masters' disciple succession. Yet, every time those relations are built at a new level and are determined by the conditions formed on the Earth. We do not need millions of followers who only show their undertaking of obligations, but do not let our Teaching into their hearts. We aspire to complete mutual understanding and collaboration with our disciples. Our messenger is just like a crutch for you during the period of time until you can go independently and get in touch with us directly. Even in this case, you will need our messenger as a lighthouse to show you the Path in the storms and gales of earthly life.

Therefore, we will go on giving our instructions in the following cycles of the dictations.[25] We ask you not to waste your time but to take all of the instructions

---

[25] At the time of the publication of this book there were more than 21 cycles of Messages, given by Masters and received by me (from March 4, 2005 until December 23, 2015). A note of T. N. Mickushina.

128

contained in our dictations not as abstract ones, but as the immediate guiding principles that you should use in your lives.

I am a very concrete Master, and I do not like to beat about the bush. Therefore, I am calling you not to wait for somebody to give you more detailed instructions for your actions. We are giving the general direction. You have to get all the details immediately from your heart.

If you reread the dictations that we have been giving through our messenger for the last year, you will understand that there is enough information in those dictations to start concrete activity. You can start with the environment around you and with the habits that you have. Do try to start not tomorrow but right now. First, free yourself from your biggest attachment that impedes you most of all in your life. That might be fear, inclination to censure and criticism, smoking, or any other attachment and any other imperfection.

Then you will find another imperfection, and then the next one. You will always know only one immediate task that you should implement. Then you will be able to start deciding the next issue.

Do not aim at too much activity at once. Take the issues that you can decide. Sometimes it is much more difficult for many to get rid of smoking than even to build an ashram.

We are calling you to follow our Path. We are telling you that the way is open. But you make your own choice, and nobody can force you to make this choice.

You are mature individuals, and we talk to you as with our equals who are just a bit behind in their advancement along the Path.

So now I say goodbye to you, and I wish you success on your Path!

I AM El Morya.

There will be those who manifest their consistency and devotion and can help us attain our goals

July 7, 2006

I AM El Morya, who has come to you again through my messenger in order to give a Teaching and talk to you about vital problems. I am glad to have such an opportunity. Every time when I come, I cannot hide my delight about the fact that there is an opportunity to communicate with you. Therefore, today, in order to save time, I am starting to report what is necessary. It is necessary for you to know about many things. If you could constantly concentrate on the goals of the Brotherhood and carry out our plans, the evolution on the planet would go at a much faster pace. Yet, you continue to reside in illusion, soothing your consciousness with the illusionary manifestations that surround you. That is why I come again and again and try to get across to your consciousness the things that are indispensable for you. You forget everything that I tell you literally right when you stop reading my messages. I have to come again and give you the same Teaching at a somewhat different angle hoping that there will be those who manifest their consistency and devotion and can help us attain our goals. It seems to you with your agile mind that you already know everything that we talk about and you go off in pursuit of new impressions hoping to occupy your carnal mind. However, you do not need any new knowledge. There is only one Teaching and one Divine Truth. This Truth can be understood only with a mind of a child. Abandonment of excess speculations and intellectual refinement is what you should do. I realize that your mental bodies are not fully developed yet. That is why you are trying to load them with various intellectual twists. You come into the gross world, and one of the goals that you come with is to develop not only your physical bodies, but also your subtle bodies: the astral body, the mental body, and the etheric body. Your subtle bodies represent your soul. Your soul needs development. That is why you will remain in the matter until you gain enough experience and until all your bodies are developed. Now the cycle is such that your mental bodies receive an impulse for development. They are curious like children and are trying to find more and more new terrains for their activity. However, in the same way as you give up alcohol, nicotine, and other attachments and habits of your physical body, you need to find the strength within you to give up the attachments of your mental body, of your carnal mind. All of your four lower bodies undergo evolution on planet Earth. You have to achieve harmony and maturity of all your bodies. Until you gain enough experience, until all your bodies gain enough experience, you cannot return to the world from which you originally had come as Divine particles. You will take the experience that you have gained to this Divine world, but only the part of your experience that corresponds to the Divine models.

So, since the mental bodies of a significant part of mankind are now going through their experiences and acquiring the necessary knowledge, you need to take that into account in your development. You have to constantly try to detect when your mind leads you into the deep forest of intellectual speculations and when you are actually coming in contact with the eternal Divine Wisdom. You should try to make your differentiation within yourselves. The Divine Wisdom does not have anything in common with intellectual speculations, which resemble some sort of a drug for your carnal mind.

Many people, when they open another message and do not see any food in it for their conceited mind, go seek that food in other places, and they receive what they are aspiring in considerable amounts. However, what is not visible to you is visible to us. We can see that what you sometimes receive and consider as being very valuable and indispensable is in the best case useless for you and, in the worst case, it pushes back the development of your soul by years and incarnations.

There are many intellectual traps into which many people of light fall. Those traps are placed so skillfully that at times it is impossible not to be caught in them if you are not constantly maintaining the attunement with our Hierarchy and asking the Ascended Masters for help. Many people rely on their own powers, on the physical muscle, and neglect the help of the Hierarchy of Light. However, this is another manifestation of the intellectual ego. At the modern stage of human development you cannot differentiate between the proper models and their malformed counterparts, between the intellectual speculations and the Divine Wisdom. That is because the difference between them can sometimes be seen only at the level of the Divine intuition and the vibrations that are natural to these manifestations.

Now I have to tell you one more important thing. It concerns your advancement on the Path of Initiations which many are trying to follow and take on responsibilities to follow that Path. Yet, in the same way as they take on the task eagerly, they turn away from the Path, whether because of their own laziness or the lack of Faith and devotion.

That is because the qualities of consistency, devotion, and determination are inherent to a very small number of individuals. As a rule, these qualities have been acquired by those individuals in their past incarnations by means of training themselves in those qualities, either in the communities of spiritual Masters or in hermit's shacks. Do not think that everything that you have in this life has been inherited by you from your parents or that you have attained these achievements yourselves in this life. Many of your attainments and qualities go back into the distant past, up to the times of ancient Atlantis and Lemuria. Only now, in this life, they come out in you, and you are given the right to use them. Therefore, please use your Divine gifts and qualities to serve the Common Good, to serve the Life on Earth, and to serve us, the Great White Brotherhood. We are the Masters of mankind that have been accompanying humanity for millions of years. We were with you during your incarnations in ancient Lemuria and Atlantis and taught you — as less developed individuals at that time — in our schools and ashrams.

Therefore, you should value what you have as your assets, your attainments that have come to you from the remote past. Use your gifts not to submerge yourselves into the illusion, but to ascend to the peak of the Divine consciousness. Do not think that you are alone on your Path. We are constantly by your side and are holding your hands in our hands. However, we cannot take you by your hand forcefully and lead you if you are like stubborn little children pulling out your hand and running away from the evolutionary path of development. Apparently, your intellectual body is not developed enough yet to conform to the Law and understand all the advantages of the Ascended Masters guiding you and helping you on your Path.

I am parting with you for today, but I am foreseeing new meetings and talks.

I AM El Morya, with hope in you.

Feel responsibility and keep your aspiration

July 19, 2006

I AM El Morya Khan, having come to you in order to give a message.

<...>

We much appreciate those who in their consciousness are able to reach the level of the awareness of collaboration with the Hierarchy. The Heaven's help that our collaborators feel at critical moments of their lives is determined by the measure of the sacrifice that they have been able to make before, serving us. We send you thoughts and wishes, and you feel the energy you need to perform the Brotherhood's affairs on the physical plane. The number of our incarnated collaborators becomes bigger and bigger. I cannot come to each of you and express my acknowledgment and gratitude for the work that you do for the Brotherhood, but I can express my acknowledgment and gratitude through this messenger. Accept my low bow. I sincerely bend down before the Light of God in you and before those of your

Divine qualities that allow you not to lose the way and to act in the interests of the Brotherhood, being on the Earth at this difficult time for the planet.

Feel responsibility and keep your aspiration. In fact, the love of constant effort and tireless application of effort distinguish our disciples. You can unmistakably identify our chelas among you. They do not whimper or complain about life, but day after day they continue doing their job for the sake of which they have incarnated. No life troubles or tests can stop them, for their Faith is strong, and their connection with their Higher Self doesn't allow them to lose the Way.

Our collaborators do not force anybody to pay attention to them. They do not tell everybody about the big work that has been completed and that is being done. No, they prefer to do their job quietly and tirelessly, without attracting excessive interest from the opposition. Everybody knows his job and does it.

Our collaborators are scattered about different countries and continents. I would like to note the special work of our collaborators in such countries as Russia, Bulgaria, Latvia, Germany, Ukraine, Lithuania, and Armenia.

We are waiting for those to appear on the land of America who will also wake up and restore their lost connection with the Hierarchy. Every new dispensation and every new opportunity that the Heavens give, offers new perspectives for those people and those countries that use that opportunity and participate in it. So, do not be shy to maintain your relations with the Russian messenger. There are no national or continental boundaries for our Teaching. We taught mankind of the Earth even when there were no signs of the continents that now exist on the planet. We will continue our training work and education of mankind, because we believe that mankind of the Earth will stand all the tests, and with dignity they will manifest those Divine qualities that are still lying dormant in most people of the planet.

We hope for collaboration with everyone; and to start your collaboration with the Hierarchy you can use my focus, my image, and every day address to me your requests and problems, your questions and wishes. The divisibility of my consciousness and the opportunity given to me by God, allows me to be present in many places simultaneously and to give you my directions and recommendations. I hear all of you who address me. You only have to learn to hear me. I come to you and speak from the silence of your heart. Try to hear me. Move away from the fuss, sit quietly in front of my image, or simply imagine me in your mind. I assure you, that if your aspiration to hear me is strong, you will certainly hear my voice deep in your heart. It won't be a human voice usual to you. It will be the answer to all your questions. You will receive the answer and you will know that I have given it to you.

Have some training. You may not hear me from the very first time. Develop your quality of communication with the fine world.

I am always with you in the silence of your hearts, but I cannot be with you unless you prepare your temples for communication with me, unless you become free of most characteristic human habits. I will list some of them: alcohol, smoking, listening to rock music, negative states of your consciousness — offence, anger, depression, self-pity, etc. — all of these prevent me from getting in touch with you on the higher plane, and prevent you from hearing me.

Don't give way to despair if you have many imperfections. If you have chosen the Path and you tirelessly go along it every day, then, very soon everything odd that impedes you will be cast away by you as useless and burdening to you on the way.

Only your Divine, eternal qualities will remain. Literally, in a few years you will look at yourself, at what you are now, and you will be surprised at how much will have been changed in you.

I am leaving you and looking forward to our new meetings in your hearts.

Well, I say goodbye to you!

I AM El Morya, always with you!

I wish you successful self-perfection

July 21, 2006

I AM El Morya Khan, who has come again.

<...>

Always remember that the Knowledge is given to you to think over, for reflection and meditation in the stillness of your heart. Do not strive to put aside the book with the dictations as soon as possible. Try to completely absorb everything that is contained in each dictation, each drop of the life-giving Divine Energy, and each Word of the Divine Truth.

We come to mankind of Earth in order to strengthen our connections, the connections between the physical and the subtle planes. Our goals and objectives depend entirely on how fully you can acquire the information and the energy that is contained in our messages.

Do not make us remind you again and again that the tremendous responsibility to transform the physical plane of planet Earth lies with you. Remember that you have come into this incarnation in order to take specific actions in the physical plane. In order for your actions to be perfect and comply with the Divine plans, you must, first of all, care about your conductors. You should tirelessly purify your subtle bodies with prayer and fasting, walks in nature, and by association with children and animals. Contemplate on beauty and under the influence of beauty you will change your inner state. Nothing has the same effect on a person as beauty and nature. Preserve and cultivate proper patterns in your lives. Try to have everything that surrounds you fill you with harmony and beauty. Do not be shy to direct other people; remind them that everything that surrounds them has a constant influence on their consciousness and inner world. This also concerns watching the television and uncontrollable listening to the radio. Safeguard yourselves from any negative vibrations from which you can protect yourselves. There are many ways to protect yourselves from negative energies, and many of those methods do not require any financial investments.

That is why I have come to remind you that everything is in your power. You can count on the help of the Masters and make the calls, but you will have to act on the physical plane yourselves. All of the wonders that happen have been carefully planned. The miracle of the transformation of the physical plane will inevitably happen, but in order for it to happen, you need to prepare that miracle in your hearts.

I wish you successful self-perfection. Make sure that not a single grain of the Divine Energy is directed to something other than its intended purpose. You are given a lot, and now you have to demonstrate your readiness to collaborate with the Heavens.

All your efforts will be multiplied and will undoubtedly germinate.

It seems that the changes that happen on the physical plane are not related to the Dictations that we give. However, believe me that almost all positive changes on the planet have always been related to the fact that people accepted our messengers and the Word that they carry. If our messengers were not accepted and honored, the country that allowed such negative actions was dropped into the twilight of consciousness for many years. We could only ask God to forgive them, for they did not know what they were doing.

We sincerely hope that the nightfall of the human consciousness has been left in the past. Ahead is the bright dawn of Knowledge that you carry in your hearts.

I have come in order to give the closing dictation of this cycle and to announce that we will continue the work through our messenger as long as such an opportunity for our work is manifested in the physical plane.

Do not forget that each of you has the responsibility to take care of our messenger. That is because Godly people have always lived thanks to the support of kind people.

I am parting with you, but I hope that our separation will not be long, and that we will meet again through this messenger.

With those of you who are ready, I will come and meet personally in the stillness of your heart.

I AM El Morya, goodbye for the moment!

We hasten to bring home to your consciousness the new tasks which need implementing

December 27, 2006

I AM El Morya, having come to you today through my Messenger.

I HAVE come!

<...>

I am glad, and all the Ascended Hosts are glad about the fact that the year 2006 has been so successful!

That is why now, right before the New Year's Eve, we hasten to bring home to your consciousness the new tasks that need to be implemented. These tasks are directly connected with the fulfillment of the plans of the Brotherhood.

As always, when a new dispensation is activated, a new Divine opportunity opens. This time the Divine opportunity is open for Mother Russia. We have been waiting for this opportunity for long decades and, finally, it is opened up. Now it is you, the currently incarnated light-bearers, who are responsible for the way this opportunity will be realized in the physical plane. We need an outpost, a place in the physical plane through which we can carry out our deeds, through which we can convey our plans and discuss with you the succession and the terms of their implementation.

I hope that next year will enable us to fulfill our subsequent plans, and, finally, we will manage to start doing practical deeds in the physical plane.

We need a publishing house which will implement our tasks and will be sponsored completely by the Great White Brotherhood.

We need an educational center where we can give knowledge on the Divine Truth on a regular basis, an educational center which will serve as a beacon in the sea of chaos that is lavishly foaming up in the life around you.

We need a Community, several communities, and as many communities as you can establish, the communities implementing the spirit of the Great White Brotherhood in the physical octave. With the help of our Communities, we will be able to introduce correct patterns and correct moral guidelines in the society.

We need people with experience in various fields in order to initiate rearrangement of all spheres of activity on the basis of Divine principles. These principles will come from the Divine world as insights and revelations. You

145

will manage to transform life very quickly in accordance with the Divine patterns if you keep your devotion and purity of your motives and aspirations.

The more your consciousness is filled with Divine patterns and Divine vision, the less room there is for the manifestation of all that is not from God and all that wishes to resist the evolutionary path of human development and leads to the maze of pseudo-culture, pseudo-divinity, pseudo-beauty, and pseudo-love.

We leave all these non-divine manifestations to the Will of God, and I think you will not ever waste your Divine Energy to sustain and feed any negative manifestations of your world. Always remember that all the energy in this Universe is concentrated in the hands of God. When you improperly use the Divine Energy given to you by God, you multiply the evil in this world.

The time has come to do Good. The time has come for you to consciously choose the Good in your consciousness and follow it in your lives, as this is the call of the time. You have been vegetating in the illusion for too long, and you have been allowed to explore your free will for too long. Now you must start the transformation of your physical world at an accelerated pace. I hope that we will work in cooperation with you and manage to do everything within the timeline, in cosmic terms, as there is no more time left. All time reserves given for returning to the evolutionary path are exhausted.

Now we are entering the narrow strip of corridor of a new cosmic opportunity, and this strip is very short. That is why all your efforts and all your energy will be required of you in order to be on time and to complete the transformation of planet Earth by the deadline that has been mentioned and affirmed.

I will not tell you the exact date when the transformations are to be completed. But I will tell you that everything will take place within the memory of one or two generations. At least, the main transformations will take place very quickly.

There are dangers on the path. There are many pitfalls and, as always, all dangers and all pitfalls arise where there is strong human ignorance. That is why you need knowledge, Divine knowledge to guide you, and you will be able to change your life and set the example for others.

All transformations will take place very quickly. Hence, I am telling you about your responsibility again and again.

Every treachery of yours that you allow postpones the term of manifestation of the Divine plan. If you have not yet considered your life from the viewpoint of the general course of evolution, then the time has come to think it over, as you exist in this Universe not on your own. You are the cells of the one organism of this Universe. That is why the success of the whole matter and the terms of its implementation depend on your proper work in accordance with the Divine plan.

Stop considering yourselves as something sepa-rated from God. Feel your oneness with all of life at least for a short while. Imagine, that on the other side of the globe people may die because of one negative thought of yours or because of a wrong choice you make.

There is always a Divine opportunity for the course of events, and there is always the worst case which becomes manifested owing to the negligence of people.

Therefore, do constantly care but not about yourselves, do care about the world. And bring into correlation everything you do with the cosmic expedience and the granted Divine opportunity.

I AM El Morya.

A Teaching on Devotion

January 10, 2007

I AM El Morya, who has come to you on this day!

<...>

There are many obvious Truths which do not even catch your eye because you think that you have heard them many times and know them well. Believe me; if you look at them from a different angle, they begin to carry a new meaning after some time. That is because you have lived through these moments of Truth in your life. Yes, there is a big difference between how you perceive the Truths when you read them and when you live them through your lives. The difference is that, when you open a Divine Truth to yourself with your heart, instead of just briefly scanning through it in a text, that Truth will never leave you. You will become the bearer of that Truth. That Truth will become inherent to you, like an integral part of your being. That is the state of your consciousness that we are trying to have you acquire. You should not be retelling old Truths, but become the bearers of Truth, the bearers of our Word and those who bring our Teaching to life.

Unfortunately, there are few people like that. Only a few of you can completely devote your lives to fulfilling our covenants, serving selflessly, having transformed your entire lives into service.

We know about you. We know each of you, who are capable of fulfilling our tasks and doing our work on the physical plane.

Each of you is under our strict control and supervision. Many of you, having received all of our trust and our credential letters, still do not find the strength to continue the work that they have started, and step away from the Path.

Every time when you come in contact with us and receive our trust, do not think that it is a coincidence. For many incarnations, you have been earning the right to even just come in contact with us and fulfill the duties that you had taken on before the incarnation.

The most pitiful situation is when you win our trust and receive the credential letters, but then you slack off in fulfilling your duties. Your mind will always gladly provide you with many logical proofs that you are right. Yet, your heart will never lie to you. Until the end of this incarnation you will always feel heaviness in your heart, the heaviness from an unfulfilled duty.

I would not want to be in your place. For there is nothing more painful in your world, not a single deed, that you could commit that would be as severe as the betrayal of your sacred work in the name of Life on Earth.

I have also come to you today to remind you of the duties that you have accepted. If, before the end of this year, you change your decision and return to the fulfillment of the obligations, your duty that you have accepted, we will defend you before the Karmic Board and try to alleviate the karmic consequences of your wrong choices in the past.

There are very few true servants who are currently incarnated. It is unbearable to watch how, one after another, they refuse to fulfill their duty and chase after the illusions of your world.

Believe me, there is nothing in your world that could be even roughly compared to the joy of service, the satisfaction that one receives from fulfilling his duty, from completing his work. When you leave the physical plane and return to the etheric octaves of Light, millions of beings of Light from the entire universe rush to show you their respect and thank you for your dedicated work during your incarnation on Earth.

Do not take for a model those who are prominent. Many of our devoted servants are waiting all their life to play their small role. That seemingly small role can at times change the situation in the whole country, and, sometimes, even in the entire world.

Therefore, listen to your heart closely. Has the time come already to manifest your service to the Life?

We will gladly provide you with all necessary assistance. We will find a way to get across to your outer consciousness the task, which should be now fulfilled.

However, when the time comes for you to act, do not whine or say how difficult it is for you and that your old wounds are sore, and that you do not have enough food reserved.

There is nothing in your world that could stop true collaborators from fulfilling their task of Life.

Therefore, try to always maintain your devotion and readiness. Train yourselves constantly. Train those internal muscles that will allow you to act when you feel like there is no more energy or capacity.

There is always room for heroism in your life. Your heroism will not be appreciated by the external consciousness of people, but your heroism will be appreciated in Heaven. For only here do they know the value of the heroic acts that you perform in the incarnation when you retain your devotion in, at times, unbearable conditions that surround you in the physical plane.

I was glad to give you this short Teaching on devotion. <...>

I AM El Morya, with Faith and Hope in you and Love to you.

Exhortations for the current day

June 22, 2007

I AM El Morya, having come to you again through my messenger.

I AM and I have come!

As always, I would like to give an exhortation that you need at this stage of your Path.

Every time I come, I wish to bring home to you my state and the tension that I experience because I apply incredible efforts to bring sometimes very important and necessary information to my disciples. I send my thoughts, I give signs, and I send angels. Every time you face my signs on the Path, for no explicable reason your mind pretends that there are no signs at all, or it considers the goings on as some misunderstanding or a coincidence.

Every time I come and every time I teach reading the signs; I cannot communicate with you verbally. The easiest way is to send signs into your world. So you have to keep your consciousness constantly at a high level. However, you lack sensitivity, the perception of the subtle realm, the sense of the subtle realm.

You easily perceive the astral plane, and you are ready to collaborate with it. But the higher planes of Being escape your attention, and external circumstances of your life shield you from the Divine levels and make the connection with our world more difficult.

I teach sensitivity and reading signs. Every time I come, I give exact instructions. Every time you listen to me, and practically in a few minutes or hours you forget what you have been told. Your consciousness switches over to the matters of your world, to your surroundings, and with the greatest consistency you escape from your own decisions that you made under the impulse of devotion and Faith, and you rush for the immediate amusements and enjoyments of your world.

It is necessary for you to learn how to keep the image of our world constantly in your consciousness. You must constantly feel that our worlds are interconnected. Every time you allow yourselves to get distracted from the reality surrounding you, cast your glance at the Heavens, and the Heavens get closer to you. Every time you concentrate too much on the illusory problems of your world, the Heavens move away from you.

Believe me, the vibrations of your world are not the same throughout the day. There are hours, especially early in the morning or late at night when the hubbub of your world calms down, and our world gets closer.

154

During these wonderful moments many of you can view angels and elementals even with ordinary human eyes.

In such minutes of closeness to our world, many people whose vibrations have not acquired enough harmony and purity, on the contrary, feel inexplicable apathy, depression, and lack of meaning of life.

Therefore, I would like to ask you to observe all situations of this kind in your life. Not so much earthly time will pass and there will be a splitting or differentiation in the population of the Earth. People with higher vibrations will perform the exodus from Sodom and Gomorrah of modern cities, cloacae of mass consciousness and low vibrations.

They will choose pure places for their settlements that still exist on the globe. Those people whose vibrations are attuned with modern cities will stay in them. Therefore, in the natural way, there will be an exodus of the people of a new Race to the Promised Land. Angels will have an opportunity to painlessly perform their work of removing from the planet all the cosmic waste incapable of further evolution.

This prophecy was given through many prophets. Every time people hear it, they continue performing their everyday activities and do not hear that in their inner consciousness. Only a small number of people, who are able to hear, appeal to the Heavens and get the signs on their Path. They aspire to the Promised Land, and this enables them to continue their evolution.

I am not frightening you, I am giving an exhortation, because right now it is the time for a sincere talk with those of you who can hear and who are ready for making concrete steps in the physical plane. I am not forcing you to give up everything immediately and rush to remote places. No, the direction of your aspiration will gradually draw Divine opportunities to you. And one day you will feel an imperceptible desire for changes, and you will change your life in accordance with the flow of Divine evolution. You are required to submit to the Higher Law and to wish to follow the Path of evolutionary development. For this you need to reconsider your life and your attitude towards life.

The reason for withdrawal from the evolutionary path is your concentration on your own self, excessive self-esteem and egoism. Therefore, what is necessary for you to develop in yourselves in the near future is the ability of self-sacrifice, compassion, and help to the people around you. When you are able to perform the deeds that are unreasonable from the viewpoint of the majority of mankind, but unselfish and filled with devotion to the Brotherhood, you are standing firmly on the Path, and we take a tight hold of your hand. You are required to reveal a little bit of unselfishness, aspiration, and devotion, and these qualities will attract to you Divine opportunities which will take you out of modern "Sodoms" and "Gomorrahs" to the path of Light and Joy.

Just think how much you win when following the Path that we are showing you and how little you are to sacrifice, only your ego and your desire to receive something for yourself.

It is necessary to raise your level of consciousness to the point when you understand that by doing something for your neighbor you actually take care of yourself. You either work off your karmic debt this way or stock up your good karma which will allow you to escape a dangerous situation instantly, just by uttering a call.

We give instructions hoping that many of you are able to perceive our words, and not just to perceive our words, but to start acting in accordance with the given Teaching.

It is the practical use of the knowledge that is of most importance. When you know the Law but do not implement it in your life, your karma does not decrease, it increases. You multiply your karma because there is such a type of karma as the karma of inactivity.[26] You have gotten this Teaching, and it means that you are able to comprehend it and to act according to it. If you do not act in accordance with the received Teaching, you evade the Path in this way. You evade the Path even when you do nothing.

Your dual world is to blame for that, the world that was created by you with those energies that you chose to spend — not on displaying Divine patterns but on getting something for yourself.

---

[26] "A Teaching on the karma of inactivity," Beloved Kuthumi, June 24, 2005. Dictations are available on the websites http://sirius-eng.net (English version) and http://sirius-ru.net (Russian version).

It is the time for transformation of your world now. The first thing you have to do is to begin acting in your life in accordance with the Teaching being given by us.

I was very abrupt and inflexible. That is because the time has changed. There is no possibility to wait any longer.

I AM El Morya Khan.

All your life must be devoted to the Divine Service

July 10, 2007

I AM El Morya, who has come to you on this day.

<...>

Now, during our future work, we would like to come even closer to you. When we are far away, your consciousness cannot fully comprehend our existence and our presence. Therefore, our task is to come closer to you, and your task is to become closer to us by raising the level of your consciousness, and then we will be able to perform work on the physical plane together.

One is afraid of the unknown. What is obscure causes fear and anxiety. Our task is to make the communication between the worlds ordinary.

We wish that there is not any shade of religion or dogma in our communication. It is time to put the association with us, the Masters of mankind, on the new foundation of collaboration and mutual help. We do not come to you for you to waste your time on reading our messages. We come to you in order to inspire you for performing work on the physical plane.

All your ordinary work should be set on the new foundation and done in accordance with the Divine principles.

It is not necessary to do anything extraordinary; you should not fear that you will come under the influence of another cult. The difference between a sect and a true Teaching is that the former creates exclusiveness for its followers. There is no exclusiveness. Anyone can become the follower of the Ascended Masters Teaching. In order to do that, you only need to carry out in your lives the Divine principles and moral behavioral patterns that we teach you.

You need to shift the accents in your daily life and do everything under a new angle — the angle of service to the Common Good, to the work of the Masters, and to the evolution of planet Earth.

There is nothing that we would want to conceal from you. The restriction of the information that you receive is solely related to the limited nature of your consciousness and the limited nature of the consciousness of our conduit, our messenger. You set this restriction yourselves because you are not trying to change yourselves, your consciousness and, consecutively, all your life, to set proper priorities in your life and act in your lives in accordance with the Teaching that we give you.

We come so that you constantly check your vibrations and the compass of your heart against our orienting points that we set for you.

If you read carefully all the dictations from the very first message that we gave through our messenger on March 4, 2005,[27] until today's dictation; if you read all of these dictations with one purpose — to understand what you should do in your lives now, you will obtain answers to all of your questions. Everything that you need is given to you. Now it is your turn. Show us that you have learned our Teaching. Show us what you are able to do on the physical plane guided by our Teaching.

Every deed on the physical plane that you perform successfully based on our principles allows us to expand the effect of this dispensation.

Therefore, think about how you can do our work collaboratively. If you need our help, write letters to us. If you need our advice, appeal to us and you will receive advice in your heart.

We are never slow to render our help. The whole question is whether you can sustain our energies that we give you to fulfill the work on the physical plane.

Every time when one of you is ready to take on the responsibility and perform our work on the physical plane, we give our blessing, our help, and our energy. You begin the work vigorously. However, only several months pass and your determination and willingness to work for God fades away. You find thousands of excuses and thousands of reasons that make you abandon our

---

[27] Tatyana N. Mickushina, *Words of Wisdom. Ascended Masters Messages.* Available from amazon.com/author/tatyana_mickushina

work and return to completing the projects that, as it seems to you, are more important and more profitable, giving something to you personally.

I am warning you — before you take on the responsibility to perform work for the Masters, please evaluate everything a thousand times. That is because we give you the energy, and if you misuse the energy that we give, if you direct it at completing your own projects, then all the energy that you use inappropriately is qualified as the karma of the unfulfilled duties before God and the Masters, or in other words, the karma of betrayal. You know that this type of karma is the hardest to work off and it is accompanied by great difficulties not only in this life, but also in several future lives.

However, if you do our work selflessly, with all your heart, then you earn tremendous good karma, and that will allow you to fulfill our tasks with even greater success in the future.

God does not want you to be poor or struggle financially. If you make proper choices and apply your efforts in the right direction, abundance will come into your life. You need to learn how to properly use and spend the Divine Energy; and if you manage to find the balance between the wise fulfillment of your personal projects and performing work for the Masters, you will never feel the shortage of energy, including the monetary energy in your life.

God requires you whole. All your life must be devoted to the Divine Service. However, there are too few individuals among you who are done with their personal karma and their ancestral karma. Therefore, you still have karmic debts left in the form of taking care of the people close to you, children, parents, and anyone with whom you have a karmic connection. This is where you need to find a wise balance between the energy that you will spend on fulfilling the work of the Masters and the energy that you direct at caring for your family and the people with whom you are connected by karma.

This is not an easy task. However, how successfully you solve it determines your future.

<...>

Thanks to all of you who support the fulfillment of our plans on the physical plane and take on the burden to perform our tasks.

I AM El Morya, until the next time!

A message to my disciples

December 23, 2007

I AM El Morya, having come to you to give the next message. The degree of importance of a particular message for you, who are incarnated on Earth, is subjective. You cannot, being on your human level of consciousness, assess the significance of the phenomenon happening, nor its importance for the further development of mankind.

Therefore, as a rule, we do not require you to make immediate and hasty decisions, nor immediate action.

To be perfectly honest, the work that we carry out continuously with the humanity of the Earth could have much better results, because the efforts exerted by us sometimes surpass all the allocated cosmic reserves. We clearly understand that it is very hard for you to look a little higher than the routine and bustle you have on a day-to-day basis. Therefore, we tirelessly come and give messages that do not show much novelty but they allow you to shake things up, and sometimes some phrase or expression in our message makes you wake up so that you become able to carry out those actions in the physical plane that are necessary and that we constantly ask you to carry out.

So, each time with a lot of patience and persistence, I ask you to start acting, not only to just read dictations, prayers, Rosaries or decrees. I ask you to implement real actions in the physical plane! Perhaps you do not quite understand what kind of actions I am talking about. I am neither asking you to overthrow the regime that exists in your state where you live, nor to make a revolution or hold a mass meeting. I ask you to do ordinary human things that you mainly do anyway. But I ask you to do these things consciously. Consider each action you do through the prism of the moral Law, the Divine Law, existing in this Universe. I ask that every day you think about the consequences of your actions and reflect on your every step.

Think of how you could ease your existence in the matter, if every move of yours was in full accordance with the Divine Law, existing in this Universe.

You would not create new karma, and you could rapidly work off your past karma by making right choices. How easy it is! It is ingeniously simple! We come and constantly tell you about the same things. But why, why don't you hear us?!

Why do you read our messages and five minutes later completely forget what you have read?! Why even during the day can't you stay under the influence of the right mental images that we send to you?

O God, it is sometimes unbearably difficult to work with embodied humanity! However, I am an optimist by nature, and I am sure that in a hundred of my dictations or in a thousand of my dictations, I will finally get a few hundred devoted disciples at my disposal that can sensitively listen to my guidance and follow my instructions. Believe me; I can see much better from my ascended state of consciousness what you should do and how you should behave.

The situation on the Earth is moving in a better direction. It is not as sad as it was a few years ago, but we would like to get greater rates of your consciousness development. A reasonable solution was found, thanks to which the rate of your development will be accelerated. We will take care that the process of energy distribution becomes more even on the surface of the Earth, so that the Earth could survive and not become subjected to destructive cataclysm. We also learned how to localize clusters of negative energies that arise in human cities. If before such clots wandered the Earth's surface and brought unforeseen changes in remote locations, now all negative karma is localized at the source of its creation, and people in their experience can assess what "stinky" things they created themselves.

Thus, by means of your states you work off more quickly what you have generated.

And that is not all! We start thinking of establishing settlements on the globe which will be free from the influence of mass consciousness. Conditions for further development of human civilization can be created in such settlements. All that does not wish to develop must ultimately be isolated and eventually cut off like a dry branch during garden work.

Everything that can grow and bear fruit should be transplanted into fresh fertile soil and blossom for the good of the evolution of planet Earth.

Such are our plans, and I share these plans with you in the hope that there are people who approach me by writing personally and asking me to be in charge of their actions to transform the physical plane of planet Earth.

However, I have to calm you down immediately. I am a very strict and demanding Master. My students are able to produce many miracles in the physical plane, but I demand full and unconditional devotion, aspiration, and discipline from them in return. Those who are not confused by my high requirements: Welcome to my classes in the subtle plane, in my retreat, where I can meet you and guide your development.

As soon as I understand that you are quite ready to become our co-worker, I will give you a task in the physical plane that you will have to implement.

As a rule, many of my disciples are eliminated immediately as soon as they get a specific assignment from me.

They are more concerned about what they will get in return. When I explain to them that they have already received all that could be obtained, the opportunity to serve the Great White Brotherhood, this answer leads them into confusion, and they go off to wander in the illusion in search of more rewards, fame, money, and other things that are more valuable in their eyes.

I know that my message will not be clear for many. However, I do not have an intention to be understood by millions. A few hundred faithful disciples are enough for me, and we will change the world in a few decades.

So, to those who are not confused by my requirements, welcome and become my disciples.

I hear every sincere appeal to me that you say in your heart. If you do not hear a reply, it is only due to the fact that you are very inattentive and too distracted by your illusion.

I have come to you today in order to give you reliable guidelines on your development.

I AM El Morya Khan.

I have come to inform you about the end of another stage of our work and about the beginning of the next one

January 10, 2008

I AM El Morya, having come to you this day.

<...>

Everyone who wishes to provide his or her aid and assistance to us is welcome! I am ready to personally consider all your concrete suggestions and to discuss the plan of actions with you.

We will inform you in the immediate future of what is being planned.

Now, I would like to orient you toward the fact that in the nearest time you will have to work seriously for the Brotherhood. I surely realize that not all of you are ready. However, I know the level of your development, and I know that there are those among you who are completely ready to take on additional commitments.

I do not demand from you that you leave everything and rush headlong to serve me.

A well weighed and planned approach is necessary. There is no need to show heroism where it is possible to work deliberately and achieve much greater results.

Then, when the time limit approaches, it will be required for you to exert all your strength and apply all of your abilities.

Therefore, you always have to be in a state of readiness for the fulfillment of the tasks we set.

Laziness, particularly with so many of you, must be defeated. I know that it is one of the qualities of Russians. Thus, I especially point out that those who are with me need to abandon this quality, overcome it, and vanquish it to the end.

Qualities of yours such as indecision, hesitation, and inconsistency are also subject to extermination. All of this must be set aside.

Great deeds are coming! Look out not to let the moment pass, so that you are not ashamed afterwards, after the end of the incarnation due to your inaction, laziness, and unresponsiveness to our call.

We call upon you for the Great Service! The most difficult thing that we encounter is the lack of people who would be able to take on the responsibility for executing our plans in the physical octave.

Many reasons and excuses are found for doing nothing, and changing nothing in your lives.

You will not be able to continue with your previous way of living. The winds of change will sweep away all the tricks of your carnal mind and all of the habitual activities of your conventional behavior.

When the mountain summit is ahead of you, there is no time to lie down and slow to a halt.

It is time to stand up and to set out on the Path!

I call you to the fulfillment of the great plans of the Brotherhood for your world!

To those of you who have regained your spirit now by reading these words of mine, I very much hope that this impulse of your soul will be with you to the end of your current incarnation. I hope that you will not go out as a candle in the wind, but will burn as a torch and illuminate the way for many, as many light-bearers have gotten lost in the illusion and are looking for their fellow light-bearers, seeking a way out of the labyrinth of illusion.

I have come to inform you about the end of another stage of our work, and about the beginning of the next one — the stage of concrete actions on the physical plane which we cannot perform without your direct participation and without your considerable help.

I very much trust in you and I am always with you on the Path.

I AM El Morya.

It is needed to go and perform the tasks of the Brotherhood now

July 1, 2008

I AM El Morya, who has come to you!

<...>

Everything that now seems unrealistic will be accomplished in the near future.

As soon as we can find a pivot point in one place on Earth, we will be able to instantly spread our vibrations to the most pure places. That is how our march around the planet Earth will begin.

The time that separates you from these events will be shortened thanks to the efforts that the light-bearers are ready to make. We will not wait for all light-bearers to wake up; we will act immediately with those who are awakened and are ready to take action under our direct supervision. There is no time to wait for those who are lagging behind. It is necessary to go and perform the tasks of the Brotherhood now. As for those who are not ready, who cannot get rid of the old burden that is pressing them towards the ground, they have only themselves to blame.

We have widely announced our plans and our current needs. Those who are ready, who joined our troops after the first call, have already begun their triumphant march towards their own Victory and towards our joint Victory, for they do not see any difference between our work and their work. We are all doing one joint work for the planet, for the future Life.

If we do not do it now, I do not want to even think about what horrifying prospect will open up for the planet.

We must use the cosmic opportunity that has been provided. We are in the good graces of the Karmic Board and the Great Central Sun. We are surprised — why are some of you still procrastinating and so sluggish in everything?

We have announced the goals that need to be achieved in the near future. We need a focus in the physical plane that will serve as a model for everyone who intends to perform the work of the Masters in the physical plane!

We will not wait until you leave all your old habits and get rid of your old attachments. The warriors of Light do not and cannot have any attachments.

However, I need to warn you that, when you leave everything and rush headlong to our call, you should stop for a minute and ask your heart whether you are not running away from your difficulties, whether you are not trying to hide behind the interests of the Brotherhood and put aside your karmic debts.

Trust me and my work experience with the mankind of Earth. None of you will be able to trick the Great Karmic Law. And, until you have balanced the necessary percentage of your karma, you will not be able to render your service to the Brotherhood. For each of your steps in our direction will make it necessary to get rid of your karmic burden. In the beginning, you will run very fast away from your karmic problems; but, when you begin your service under our supervision, your karma will begin to return to you so quickly that you will have to face one karmic situation after another. If your karmic baggage is too heavy, soon thereafter you will run headlong back home, and until the end of your incarnation you will wonder what it was that had happened to you.

Therefore, it is necessary to hurry, but it is also necessary to carefully analyze the degree of your readiness.

Sometimes, well thought-through and planned actions are much more important than those that are rushed and done fast.

It is necessary to evaluate the situation all the time. There is no one recipe for all. Everyone has his or her own karmic situation; therefore the recommendations in each case will be different. Therefore, make haste slowly. This will be the right directive that you should follow in your lives.

Our long-term and devoted disciples know and understand too well what I am talking about. For sometimes, it is better to evaluate everything carefully, than to rush headlong into something. Yet, in another situation, one should actually leave everything and run after the first call, as there will be no second call.

I take on the responsibility to guide you in your choices, if you ask for my help. However, when you ask me for help and ask for my advice, do not shut your ears to my advice. I will talk to you with signs that are comparable to the rustling of leaves or a quiet breath of wind.

I have come to you on this day to attune you to the necessity of rendering the service that you came to do in this incarnation. I am glad that the purpose of my visit has been fulfilled.

I AM El Morya, and goodbye until we meet again!

The severity of the moment obliges me to warn you about what is happening

December 29, 2008

I AM El Morya having come to you again!

I have come on one of these final days of the year, and there are certain reasons for this — reasons of planetary nature. I would like to remind you that last year the decision was made that the vibrations of the physical plane of the planet Earth should be raised.[28] This decision may have slipped your mind without any trace.

It is very strange to hear about some decisions of the Higher Cosmic Council among the holiday fuss and muddle. It is not clear how this decision will affect the lives of each of you.

As a matter of fact, at that time two years ago this news did not manifest itself, and you decided that something must have been confused up there.

---

[28] Dictation "An important Message," The Presence of the One, December 28, 2007. Dictations are available on the websites http://sirius-eng.net (English version) and http://sirius-ru.net (Russian version).

176

Many of you may have expected that raising the vibrations of the physical plane reminded you of something festive, noisy, and joyful.

Let me explain to you the situation the way I see it and the Ascended Masters interpret it.

Your world as a community of incarnated individuals had failed to climb the next step of evolutionary development on your own. Each of you preferred hiding and enjoying your lives in your snug holes.

Therefore, a decision was made to hurry you a little bit, and the vibrations of the physical plane of the planet Earth slightly rose. A year passed, and this change of vibrations started affecting your lives. It doesn't concern a certain country, and it doesn't concern a certain individual or a group of people. It is a global event that will affect the lives of all people living on the planet Earth.

Some people will not tolerate the rising vibrations, and they will make a transition; somebody will be ailing, and somebody's psychological problems will worsen due to the rising of vibrations. The worst thing happens when the fates of states get into the hands of people with an unbalanced psychic set-up and whom we will be unable to influence because they have chosen to be influenced by forces opposing us. That is why there is a danger of wars, of acts of terror, and of any actions of people trying to settle matters in an old fashion, and not realizing that the time has changed.

That is why balancing these actions are necessary and essential. We are trying to do it, but we need your help. Your hands should be stretched and they will be met and something will be put into them.

The world financial system does not correspond to the new time, and if it doesn't change its approaches in the nearest future, and doesn't try to adjust to new requirements, the world economy is in for a crisis that mankind hasn't come across yet throughout all its observable and described history.

You have things to consider in these last days of the departing year. I can prompt you what to undertake. You need to find a point of quietness and tranquility, of calm and peace inside of you in which God abides. From this point you should try to realize that there is nothing in your physical world that can harm you and harm your soul unless you wish to succumb to panic mood and rush to save yourself and give way to your mood.

You have no place to run to. You cannot collect your belongings and evacuate from the planet. You will have to tolerate everything up to the end. You will have to put up with what can happen and is happening already. On my part, I can tell that you are given a chance and everything is going very slowly. That is why practically each of you can influence global processes in progress. The more people that are capable of preserving imperturbability and peace of the mind, the stronger your faith is, the easier way everything will develop and occur.

You must believe now that no forces can harm your souls until you are sure of your invulnerability.

It is time for your active actions.

You cannot pretend that nothing is happening. You will find all your former pastimes and toys absolutely useless, and you will be amazed at the time you wasted. You must make up the leeway. Those of you who are ready to act for the benefit of the planet Earth evolutions, those of you who are ready to wake up the sleeping ones and to take them out of the house ablaze, my appeal is namely to you today.

Hurry up. Little time is left. We are waking those who still can be wakened. We are doing everything we can. Are you doing everything you can?

Are you capable of waking up and directing at least one soul in your surroundings?

Many of you are sleeping so soundly that you are aware of nothing. It is a pity because the time of cosmic opportunity is coming to the end. The question is in the number of souls that can be saved. Every soul counts and the time has never been so short.

I have come on this day so that you might realize the complexity of the situation. Try to realize that your invulnerability is directly connected with your Faith and devotion, with how much you can obey the Divine Law in effect in this universe.

I do not frighten, but the severity of the moment obliges me to warn you about what is happening and to give into your hands a rescue rope of opportunity.

I AM El Morya.

The time of training is over; the time is ripe for practical classes in action yoga

January 5, 2009

I AM El Morya, having come to you this day!

I have come today to sum up a certain work done so far and to outline our plans for the future.

In whole, we are satisfied with the work performed on the physical plane. We are very glad, and we greet the warriors of Light around the entire world that responded to our call and helped us to accomplish the plan — building the Ashram of our messenger, and starting up a civic organization and a publishing house.

We are very delighted!

However, I have come to ask you not to relax, since everything done so far is just a very initial, first little step in the right direction. Do not think that everything has been attained. Much more than you have done is still waiting ahead. I must warn you that further movement will be associated with greater and greater difficulties.

Thus, all of your vigilance and all of your attention will be required.

We are entering the stage that can palpably show that the world as a whole is heading for the wrong way, the way of satisfying the ego, the way of attachments, the non-divine way.

That is why what we are doing with the help of our messenger and with your help and participation can be disliked by many people: those who do not desire any changes, those who got used to acting in old ways.

Consolidating and uniting on new principles all warriors of Light who are ready into a single world Community becomes indispensable.

On the physical plane you can build settlements and even create free-standing villages. All is in your hands. But always remember that the key issue is forming the Community in the spirit.

Karmic circumstances are not favorable for every-one. Not all of you can put on a girdle and start on a journey at the first summons. Unfortunately, that karma and those karmic obligations that you have to your family should be solved and untied first thing.

You must not have debts to society and settle in our Communities. You must not push aside your children and rush to head off into the future.

You will not make a decent community member without solving your family problems and your inner problems.

Yes, we need a model, a pattern to follow on the physical plane. But, to organize this model clean hands and pure hearts are needed.

Any spot on your clothes will be multiplied in the minds of ignoramuses, and they will be telling others all over the world how untidy you are and how you fail to keep even your clothes clean.

That is why the primary concern becomes the problem of finding those who are ready and who by their past incarnations have already proved their devotedness to the Great White Brotherhood, and in this incarnation they have succeeded not to encumber themselves with an excessive karmic burden.

Such community members are capable of forming the Community backbone, and on their arrival at the Community all others will be eager to follow their models in behavior, in conducting affairs, and in keeping the house developed by these pioneers.

You are to start from scratch. There are no models we could recommend to imitate. There is a theory, whole volumes in developing communities, but there is nobody to implement these guidelines into practice.

I will stand guard over my Community and I will be with you in all your affairs. I will be able to stand up for our stronghold, for our outpost on the Earth. But all of this being said does not mean that you should rely heavily on me and on God for everything. You will have to roll up your sleeves and to perform all of the necessary work on the physical plane by yourselves.

I will provide you support in the thinner plane. I will defend you from encroachments by those possessed with malicious entities and flying into a rage at the mere mentioning of the Community. But it is you who will have to put these raging ones into hospitals and will have to worry about keeping the Community safe from such inhuman monsters.

I warn you about what can be and what obstacles you can come across on your way.

Thus, do not celebrate the victory when you have not come out into the field for a battle yet. You may not reach your destination.

It is too early to repose on one's laurels and to muse on rest. Our affair is in full swing. All your vigilance, promptness, and efficiency are required for you not to drop a brick and not to get stuck in the cobwebs of bureaucratic and functionary tricks.

Now the battlefield has moved to officials' rooms, to courts, and inspectorates. Therefore, you will be required to have a knowledge of laws and knowledge of case administration.

It was simpler when everything was settled in the battlefield. The enemy was facing you and looking you straight in the eye. Now you are smiled at by everyone, but they do their deeds of evil in their sleeves. You do not know in what room a snake of envy or a scorpion of revenge is lurking.

The time of training is over; the time is ripe for practical classes in action yoga.

Show what you are capable of and the way you keep the covenants of the Masters in the fuss of everyday routine and in the bureaucratic muddle.

There is much for you to do ahead. Nothing similar has been intended yet.

There exists a plan and it is to be accomplished!

Are there any volunteers among you?

I AM El Morya.

We continue the mission that we have started in Russia

July 10, 2009

I AM El Morya.

Have you been waiting for me? I know that many of you have been anxiously waiting for my coming since none of the Masters speaks so decidedly and concretely as I do.

The responsibility for the whole mission that we are starting in Russia rests on me. My responsibility makes me speak succinctly, concretely, and to the point. It is necessary to discuss a lot within the limits of one message.

So, I will start then. You might know that our mission in Russia is stuck. And you may know that the reason for that is the sluggishness of those light-bearers who were to be involved in our mission but instead found other activities for themselves and started doing something that is far from our interests.

For what a long time and how thoroughly our missions of Light are prepared! How many discussions are held in the higher plane with the souls preparing for those missions!

Once you approach the time when actions are needed something that is impossible to program beforehand happens: you are carried away by something that you were never interested in before and believe that you have incarnated precisely for that. You do not hear and do not want to hear any of our words that you read in the messages or hear in the retreats during your nightly dreams; you do not see any signs in the physical plane, you are just caught up in the illusion.

So what is left? I applaud the heroic efforts of our messenger. It will not be a secret to you if I say that it was not in the least planned that this woman would be involved in the construction and would dedicate the invaluable days of her incarnation to the things that were to be done by other people.

I applaud, but at the same time I have to say all fine and dandy, but instead of advancing forward during those two years while the construction was in progress we have stepped several years back.

Yes, we are forced to put you at a desk of the first class and start our training again instead of doing those things that have been planned.

We expected to make greater progress, but we will not put the cart before the horse. We will be waiting until the Russian man has gotten enough sleep and half rises from his stove-bench.

There is a proverb: "The Russians harness slowly but drive fast." I have to say that you have not even started to harness yet.

We are right at the beginning of the path and are urgently seeking replacements for those individuals who volunteered to take part in this mission of Light but did not stay the distance. Each person has his own reason, but the overall result is deplorable. Isolated lights, flashing here and there, cannot serve as an indicator of success. And instead of rallying under the banner of our messenger, you have found a pretext for yourselves in the form of different assignments that you try to undertake in the physical plane here and there.

There cannot be any other assignments for you than those of the Brotherhood.

When we sound full-blast the full-scale attack, you cannot be playing the harmonica. But, that is exactly what many things you do look like.

Instead of taking part in our mission and helping us, you have found many activities that are perhaps good at a certain stage of evolutionary development but in no way suitable for your souls.

It is the same as if an alpinist who has conquered many of the highest peaks of the world will be climbing an ice-hill down which five-year-old children slide in winter. I do not know what other words I can find to reason with you.

Nevertheless, we continue the mission that we have started in Russia. We will be moving just as much

187

as will be possible. I am sad. We could have achieved much more.

However, it is early to strike the balance; the work is quite far along. And when we are able to unfurl our banners and deploy our troops, we will see who will dare to set off their ingenious ploys and mercantile interests against us.

The time has come to build up our power in the physical plane.

We say time and again that it is necessary for you to perform concrete actions and to perform them not chaotically but in an organized way. Becoming a union is necessary for you. As soon as we can implement what we planned in one place of the globe, we will be able to easily repeat that experience in many places.

I expected more promptness and vim from you. Well, we will try to restructure our battle lines and continue augmenting the potential of Light. You have been waiting a long time for my coming. However, I cannot afford the time to talk to you for long.

Do work better, and I will devote more time to you!

I AM El Morya.

I wish to instill confidence in you and liberate you from fear

January 21, 2010

I AM El Morya. I foresee the cheerful shouts of my chelas "At last!"

Yes, beloved, I have come!

<...>

You finally have to take full responsibility for everything that takes place on the planet. You have to stop acting like children and grow up.

During all my incarnations, the top priority and importance for me was to fulfill the Will of God. I carried out the principles of brotherly relationships during my incarnation as King Arthur. It was unusual for those times. Yet, we tried to resolve all evolving arguments and internecine conflicts at the round table. I acted in accordance with the Divine principles and taught these principles to others.

During my incarnation as Akbar the Great, my politics were based on respect for the beliefs of other people and nations. Still, during those times there were enough people who wanted to divide and take the power in their hands.

Yet, I used my position of the emperor to carry out the Divine ruling principles into life.

During my incarnation as the Rajput prince Morya, I also used all of my powers to elevate the consciousness of people to a higher Truth, to demonstrate the limitations of human consciousness, and to raise the consciousness of those individuals who were ready for it.

Now I am fulfilling the same mission: carrying out the Will of God, the Divine principles into your world.

It is not always successful. The times change and so do the means of working with people's consciousness. Yet, I do not lose hope that, sooner or later, the Divine principles will win in all aspects of human life!

Our new messages have become spread the most in Russia. People's reactions to them are different. Yet, one can see more and more clearly the main trend of how the given Teachings are applied to life. Even when nothing real gets done and when people just read our messages with a good positive mindset, even then they influence the life of the society, including its economy and politics. Yes, beloved, the influence of our energies contained in the messages takes place beyond your consciousness, beyond your carnal mind. We pour the nectar of the Divine Energy into your hearts, into the hearts of those who are ready. While passing through your lower bodies, the Divine Energy is capable of having an influence on everything that surrounds you.

First of all, it changes your consciousness. This is what we are not tired of talking about and what we are trying hard to achieve, because when people are at a higher level of consciousness, they cannot accept many of the things that they could in the past. One person, who is capable of keeping his consciousness at a relatively high level, maintains balance within the radius of several kilometers from the place where he lives.

We will attain our goals no matter what. In the past we expected that those individuals who incarnated with a certain mission would finally lift up their heads and begin to do what they were meant to do in this incarnation. Now we act at a much larger scale. We raise the vibrations of the entire physical plane, so people have to act in accordance with the Divine examples, because old behavioral stereotypes do not bring the same results any more.

To keep up with the times you will have to get rid of the old load that lies on your shoulders as a burden that does not let you take a single step forward. Be brave and throw aside all your attachments, your habits, all that lowers your vibrations. You will understand where to go and what to do as you go. When one is light on his feet and flexible in his thoughts, it is easier for us to guide him in his actions and supervise him, especially when he himself asks for the Divine guidance for his life.

Do not be afraid to lose your belongings and attachments. Your potential for future existence as an individual lies on one side of the scale while all your lovely attachments are on the other side.

These are incompatible things. Your belongings do not have any value if you look at them unbiased from the highest point of view. All of them are valuable only for your carnal mind. Your fears of the upcoming changes do not have any grounds. If you go in line with God and the Masters, you are not afraid of any changes that are to come.

We counted on an easier path. You chose the most difficult one. Well, it is your choice, but even if it is this lowest path, you need to move along it. There is a Russian proverb: "No water runs under a lying rock." ("No pain, no gain.") So go ahead and begin taking steps; you will orient yourselves and adjust the course as you go.

As long as God lives in your heart, as long as you are cheerful and friendly, and as long as you believe and love, you will not be afraid of anything!

I wish to instill confidence in you and liberate you from fear with the help of today's message.

Leave the past behind you. The New Day and the new Divine opportunity await you!

I AM El Morya!

We give our helping hand to everyone who asks us for help

June 05, 2010

I AM El Morya.

<...>

It has never happened that the Ascended Realm left humankind to themselves. It is a very big illusion of the human consciousness that mankind is able to develop on their own according to their laws that have no connection with the Law of this Universe. There is one cosmic Law for this Universe, and one of the points of that law is about the help from those who have achieved more on the path of evolution to those who achieved less. That is why the Ascended Masters and I do everything that is possible in the current conditions. Those of you who believe that you are spiritually developed and advanced, why don't you follow our example? It seems to you that serving the evolutions is certainly something high and joyous that will take you to a podium and put a crown with laurels on your head.

You are mistaken, beloved. In most cases, 99 percent of our work and the work of our incarnated collaborators is usual routine work. There is a difference between those people who do the same job living their usual life and our collaborators. The main distinctive moment will be the incentive with which you do your work. Why do you do your work?

Ninety-nine percent of the people who read our messages will say, "In order to earn money, of course."

Only one percent and even less, who have achieved the next step of evolution in their consciousness, will say that they do their job for the Common Good, for the whole mankind and for Serving the whole Life.

That difference in the incentive leads to the fact that most people are involved in karmic activity whereas our collaborators who work for Common Good create good karma for the whole mankind, and it can be used for regulating the process of evolution on the Earth.

For many of you, I am saying incomprehensible and mysterious things. However, the attitude toward your work is fundamental. The incentive that underlies the basis of your work changes the result of the efforts that you apply.

That is the sense of what was said,[29] that the two men will be in the field; one is taken and one is left.

---

[29] "Then two men will be in the field; one is taken and one is left. Two women will be grinding at the mill; one is taken and one is left." (Matthew 24:40-41).

Two women will be grinding at the mill; one is taken and one is left. Because the result of your work will be directed either to multiply illusion, and in this case in your consciousness you are not ready to pass to the new leap of the evolutionary development, or on the contrary, with your work you strengthen the New Life, the new step of the evolutionary development, and you are ready for that step. Your consciousness has ripened to pass to the new step of evolution.

Your consciousness is changing first of all, and your attitude towards work in particular. That is why I have come, and I hope I will come again in the future in order to give you that simple truth that is obvious to such an extent that it is clear even for a child, but for some reason it always slips away from your field of attention.

So your attitude toward work and the incentive that moves you is a very important moment.

In essence, it determines the further direction of your development. The Divine opportunity that is given to you with these messages urges you to have the right guidelines, the right direction of your motion.

<...>

We do not urge you to believe blindly. We call you to move higher to the level of consciousness at which you can experience the true Faith — not the faith that is imposed from the outside, but the one that comes from your hearts. Only in this case, we reach the result we aspire to. Because the man that truly believes can take the next evolution step.

Everything is interlaced in your world. Your karmic debts separate you from the state in which your doubts, uncertainty, and fears vanish.

We give our helping hand to everyone who asks us for help and who is sincerely aspired. You fence yourselves off from the stretched helping hand and prefer to sink into the sea of illusion because of your egoism and absence of Faith.

So, always remember that I will throw my lifeline to everyone who will ask me about it sincerely. Do not hesitate to appeal and ask for help, and then our help will definitely come!

I AM El Morya!

Not going wide but moving deep you reach

December 23, 2010

I AM El Morya!

Urgency dictates the transmission conditions of our messages.

The time is short and there is much that should be said. There is much to be warned about.

It seems that the world is the same. The seasons, days and nights change the same way. However, the situation on the planet Earth changes imperceptibly. We have come. We have warned.

Still, the only panacea that you might need for all human diseases at this historic moment is the change of your consciousness.

It is exactly the change of your consciousness, but sometimes it is not your understanding of the meaning of changing of your consciousness.

It seems to you that if you read the Masters' dictations, carry out prayer vigils or read Rosaries, you change your consciousness. Let me mention that it is not always like that because a set of mechanical actions, some number of prayers or books read, cannot serve as sufficient evidence that you are moving along the Path.

Your physical world possesses a quality of duality. The same actions can lead either to a positive result in terms of evolution or to a negative one.

Any action on the physical plane possesses duality. The same actions can lead either to a good result or to a catastrophe.

For example, you carry out a prayer vigil. You spend much time every day. From the point of view of the majority of people, you perform a good deed that will certainly benefit the world. However, your actions can also be directed to the opposite course. Even reading prayers sincerely you can create karma. It is because your motive drives the energy.

My words seem incomprehensible to many people. Praying itself is still an impossible result for many people.

We are speaking about finer things that are not accessible to everyone. In all its seeming simplicity, this Teaching that we are giving is the most difficult Teaching existing on the globe at the given time because this Teaching opens the doors to the Eternal Life for you. But only those who can entirely adopt this Teaching will get the keys to the door leading to Eternity. Not only the keys, but that very door leading to Eternity will be hidden from the rest who take from our Teaching what suits them and throw away the rest like useless rubbish.

Pride, including spiritual pride, is what moves many so-called seekers of truth. They think that they possess wisdom that allows them to combine different teachings and religions for their spiritual move to the Truth.

Do not find comfort in the illusion! Thoughtless and blind combination of different teachings has never led to any positive result.

Humanity is at the stage of its evolutionary development at which it cannot see the Truth which is right in front of their face, but it chases shadows that loom on the other side of the globe as if they were the panacea for troubles.

The Truth is only several centimeters away from your hand if you put your hand on your chest in the heart area. The more you chase after different information and try to make a synthesis of different teachings, the farther you will go away from the Truth.

Not going wide but moving deep you reach...

You can visit many beautiful places, temples, cities, and museums. You can waste all your life on that. But you will be able to reach the peak of the Divine consciousness as long as you head for the peak.

There is not any quantity of information, which absorbed in incredible amounts, can bring you closer to the Truth. Because the Truth is simple, and common illiterate people listening to Jesus' homilies were able to understand the Truth.

You waste so much energy and strength visiting different seminars, reading volumes of literature, but in the end, all that information lies as an insurmountable obstacle between you and the Divine Truth. That is because you forget the main thing: why you need that information. Even if at the very beginning of your way you had the true motive, wandering in the information labyrinths you forgot why you went there.

It seems to you that intelligence and spiritual wisdom will bring you closer to the Divine Wisdom. However, quite the opposite thing happens: the greater your intelligence is, the farther you are from the Divine Wisdom. The human wisdom, as the basis of a happy and long life on the Earth, cannot help you when you attack the Peak of the Divine consciousness at the breaking point of your strength.

Only through renunciation; only through self-sacrifice; only through disinterested giving of all your strength serving your neighbor, can you move along the Divine Path. But, from the point of view of the majority of mankind, everything that we speak about is just fine slogans which they read condescendingly and even applaud.

The situation becomes strained. Everything is not changing in a favorable direction. The period has come when each of you, who are reading these lines, has to risk and throw away the illusive wellbeing and dare to climb nude rocks. Only inner barriers separate you from the Truth.

I am speaking allegorically. What you have to do is make truly revolutionary changes within yourselves.

<...> In order to make your prayer effective, pray as if your child was on fire, and his rescue and life depends only on your prayer.

It was nice meeting you again. I hope for future meetings!

I AM El Morya!

An ability to admit

June 26, 2011

I AM Morya.

I have come again through our messenger!

Beloved, today I have come to affirm the principle of Divine guidance in your minds and hearts, since there is nothing in your lives more important than following and obeying God's Will.

This simple Truth can work miracles on all the planes of Existence when it takes hold upon a human individual.

You are limited by the frames of matter and the laws operating within matter only until you raise your consciousness and progress on to the Divine level of consciousness. All the limitations of the material world vanish at this level of consciousness, and you escape towards the freedom of the universe.

Myself and the other Ascended Masters are trying to bring this simple Truth to your consciousness, because this process of comprehension of the

Divine Truth is the most important. As soon as your consciousness admits that there is another world, and this world is open for the exploration of your inquisitive mind, then immediately, new opportunities inspiring you to explore the New World and new experiments open up in your life.

Do not be afraid of what is coming up for you, as what is still in store for you is more joyful and inspiring than everything that surrounds you in the physical world. It is exactly an ability to admit the prospects of a new life within your being that will make it possible for you to surmount many of the imperfections, habits, and attachments characteristic of you at present.

Your aspiration and desire to rise to the new level of comprehension of the Divine Reality can work miracles in your lives.

So do dare! The Path is open! All you need is to take the first step and go to great lengths to get ahead!

When your mind impedes you and points to any impossibility and circumstances, you should know that all the obstacles and all the circumstances are surmountable with the help of God and the Ascended Hosts.

Therefore, your Faith — Faith and Love — this is what should always be with you. This is what should guide all your actions and deeds in the physical plane.

Common sense and intellect are guided purely by human logic. From the point of view of human logic, many things that we are talking about and that we are directing you toward are illogical.

However, we are calling you to be guided by the Divine logic. For this logic there are no limits or obstacles in the physical world.

You imagine that water is solid like rock, and you walk on the water.

You imagine that you are lighter than air and you fly.

You imagine that you are rising to a new level of consciousness, and you are on the new level of consciousness.

Everything is surmountable; everything is possible with God!

Therefore, the qualities of Faith, aspiration, and constancy are irreplaceable for you at this stage of your development.

What man is unable to do, God can do; even that which seems impossible from the point of view of human logic.

Just let God into your consciousness and the rest He will do Himself.

It is uncomfortable to repeat these simple Truths. However, bustle and the conditions of your life are constantly hiding from you the perspectives that we are revealing in our messages.

Therefore, every day you should literally drag yourself out of the swamp of mass consciousness and aspire to the heavenly peaks of the Divine consciousness. One day missed by you puts your clock back for one week.

Thus, only your daily work upon yourself, only your everyday efforts can change you and the illusion around you.

Do not think that changing everything can be done quickly. Each of you is on his part of the Path. For one it is enough to apply a small effort to mount the pass from which there opens a view of the peak of the Divine consciousness; others will have to go through a thick forest of karmic mistakes and delusions of the past.

So, do not relax even for a minute. Each of your daily efforts in incarnation equals a thousand years of efforts that you apply in the higher world between incarnations.

Do not waste even a minute of your stay in the dense world. Believe me, that it is the very time now when each day of your aspirations transfers you to the future of the New Day in quantum leaps.

Do not pay attention to the people around you. Each of them chooses his own future. It is impossible to make anyone aspire to God. A premature contact with the Light of our Teaching can be as unbearable for some souls that dwell in the darkness of illusion as a contact with the bright light of the day for a person who has just come out of a dungeon.

Eyes should get used to the Light. A soul should be aching for the real world in order to set out on the Path. Then none of the temptations of the illusory world and none of the obstacles can overcome the Spirit of a person who has broken away from the dungeon of the dense world and rushed to the Light that he already sees within his being.

Your planet is taking in more and more new energies of revitalization — the energies of new vibrations. These energies are rousing more and more souls and making them wake up and stretch with pleasure, anticipating the New Day.

The arrival of the New Day, new consciousness, and the transition to the new reality is inevitable for those who are able to wake up, for those who are still alive.

Sooner or later, the soul of a person will make him rise and set his heart on his return journey back to the real world.

Today I have come to give you an impulse of my energy, to give you the right direction of movement and ingrain hope for the New Day into your being!

I AM El Morya!

I am clearly showing you the Path and the direction of your advancement

January 2, 2012

I AM El Morya!

<...>

Very soon those hidden keys and the new energies that we have managed to transmit into your world with the help of our messages will be revealed. It will happen inevitably and regardless of your external consciousness.

The miracle that we have spoken about requires preparation. We have dropped into your consciousness those grains of the Divine Wisdom that will inevitably germinate. It will be like a miracle.

Not all the grains sowed by us will be able to germinate, as not all of the souls are ready for the seeds of the Divine Wisdom to germinate in them. However, I must note for you that there are not so few of those who have prepared themselves, their souls, for all this time while we have been giving the dictations through our messenger. A sufficient number of those of you, who have been reading and rereading our messages on the regular basis for these seven years, have reached a necessary and sufficient level of consciousness in order to move to the qualitatively other level of development.

We have foreknown that not everything will be successful. We have expected more. But even what we have now is enough.

With satisfaction, we state the important fact that those still hidden processes of the consciousness development of the best representatives of humanity are progressing in the right direction and at a stable rate!

I must tell you with all the certainty and clarity that the age has come when only those individuals who have managed to perceive our Teaching, will be able to continue the evolution on planet Earth successfully. No matter how few of you there are here, we hope that our sprouts will not keep us waiting.

It is difficult to imagine now that everything may change. However, it will exactly be so, and it will be like a miracle.

Be brave to aspire with your consciousness to the new and the unusual! Do sweep away all the old and moribund things! When you are able to do it — bravely and decisively — the new and the newest will instantly come to your world.

Nature abhors a vacuum. As soon as you make a decision to free yourself from any of your negative qualities or habits, you will be able to attract a Divine and perfect quality to replace that imperfection. And so, giving up the old, you advance the new into your world. Aspiring to lofty things, you replace old and moribund things with them.

Do dare! Right now your aspirations will be welcomed and positively supported by Heavens! For the time has come! The time has come for great transformations! The time has come for the cycle to turn. Very soon you will rise on the wave of cosmic energy to the Divine level of consciousness necessary for humanity at this stage.

Then, when your consciousness is able to rise to the Divine level, all the necessary transformations in all the spheres of life of the society will occur as if by themselves.

The average level of consciousness determines all the spheres of life in the society. It is exactly the society, where fear, aversion, hatred, and anti-love prevail, that can produce armaments and fix borders.

The society, where love and harmony prevail, opens the borders; and the Divine Freedom has an opportunity to manifest itself where only yesterday chaos and fear reigned.

Be brave! It is just impossible that things can be worse than they are now. Non-divine manifestations will be forced to leave your physical world very soon.

And now, when you are puzzled in which direction you are to move and where to aspire, I am clearly showing you the Path and the direction of your advancement.

Only the veil in your consciousness does not allow you to understand my words and to assimilate the simplest notions of the Divine world.

Be brave to give up festive tinsel and artificial lights. Come out to the open space of the universe!

Do discover distant worlds for yourselves; do climb the dazzling snow-white summits of the Divine consciousness within yourselves!

You have things to do! You have a lot of work now! Do start your advancement! All that you need has already been given. All the guidelines are given; all the reefs and hidden streams are shown.

Do start going! Forward!

I AM El Morya!

It is necessary to start acting!

December 28, 2012

I AM El Morya!

Urgency dictates today's Message.

I have just left the session of the Karmic Board in order to share the recent news of this meeting with you.

Well, the results of the year have been summed up. I must note for you that, on the one hand, the results are joyful, as we have found that the transition of the vibrations of planet Earth has been successful! We managed to avoid cases of emergency. And it makes us happy!

On the other hand, there is something that makes us sad. You can probably guess what it is. We have expected more promptness, more consciousness and more devotion from our chelas who are incarnated now.

During the last few years we have managed to achieve almost the impossible: we have created and anchored the outpost of the Brotherhood, the outpost of Light in the physical plane of the land of Russia. Right in

211

the middle of Russia! Hitherto, it was an unprecedented victory! This took place in 2007.

What happened afterwards cannot serve as a model. To our general regret, the light-bearers of Russia could not withhold the outpost of the Brotherhood. The land of our Messenger's Ashram has continuously been attacked by the opposing forces during all these five years. We could hardly repel one attack after another. As for the rest of the regrettable situations connected with the Ashram of our Messenger, you have been timely informed through our Messages. I myself have come many times and literally begged and asked you for help.

Instead of help, we saw the petrified hearts of our former flaming followers. One after another the light-bearers withdrew from our Messenger, and many of them committed the worst crime — a betrayal.

The result did not fail to come: We lost those advantages that had been created in the Russian land. We lost the rates of the advancement, and now we are forced to reap the fruits of the lack of promptness, of the laziness, and the betrayal.

Was it truly so far beyond your strength to join together and to withstand the attack? Is the burden of Light so heavy?

It is a pity that the window of the Divine opportunity that has been open for Russia all this time is closed.

I foresee the mood of panic of many of our disciples who will read and reread this Message of mine.

I foresee the wave of doubts and negative surges.

Is this a dignified bearing for our disciples? Do we, the Ascended Masters, really teach you to behave in this way?

Yes, the Karmic Board confirmed that the Divine opportunity for Russia is closed, and a veto is imposed upon the transmission of the Messages of the Masters in the land of Russia.

Our authentic disciples consider the failure as an opportunity to learn from the mistakes. Our authentic disciples cite their unity and oneness against any attack of the opposing forces.

There is a reason for you to unite! There is an assignment that needs to be fulfilled!

With the help of your efforts and thanks to the flame of your hearts, a new opportunity can be open. Show your unity! Demonstrate your willingness to sacrifice your momentary hobbies and games in the illusion for the sake of the Masters' mission!

Why are there so few authentic and devoted warriors under our banners? Where have all the knights and heroes gone, those who took the responsibility for the protection of our Messenger before the incarnation?

Hey! Where are you?

Is your lot truly so heavy? Is it not the time to remember your obligations and your duty?

I am not speaking about those who have betrayed and gone. I address those who are still bearing the burning spark of devotion and the flame of Divinity.

Do show your determination to serve the Masters, and the Karmic Board will consider the Divine opportunity for Russia again.

Now we are forced to give our Messages in completely different countries.

This time we have been giving our cycle of the Messages in Portugal. The last cycle of our Messages, as you remember, was transmitted by us in Latvia.

Well, God can draw positive moments in any situation. If the light-bearers failed to take our banner on time and spread our Teaching all over the world, then we will do it ourselves.

You know that during the reception of our Messages a great deal of Light is released. And this is the main reason for which we give our Messages. Therefore, many countries of the world now have a chance to create conditions for our Messenger necessary for the reception of our Messages. A more even distribution of the energy around the globe is welcomed!

At the end of my Message I would wish to confirm for your consciousness the inevitability of the changes that are coming forth.

And the faster you will be able to master the Teaching being given by us, the more rapid will be the rates of changes in all the spheres of life of human society.

To start with, remember that once and for all, everything that concerns the mission of Light in the physical plane is liable to your full care and responsibility. Imagine an envoy of a different country who has encountered misunderstanding and the demonstration of obvious animosity on the side of the authorities and the population of the country where he serves as the envoy. I think that there is not any country in the world that can ignore the manifestation of animosity towards their representative. We, The Ascended Hosts, cannot ignore the manifestation of animosity towards our Messenger either. Many times the Teaching was given on the karma that appears at the manifestation of any negative actions directed against our representative on the Earth, our Messenger.

Any karma can be worked off in the easiest way if you admit making a mistake and apologize. But if ignorance and arrogance do not allow people to admit their mistakes and to repent of them, then the negative karma starts to manifest in the physical plane in the form of different cataclysms, social coups, and financial disasters.

Therefore, you have no time to sit on your hands. It is necessary to start acting! Do not be afraid of creating karma with your incorrect actions. If your motive is right, then regardless of how incorrect your actions seem to be at the current historical moment, God will always be able to straighten out the situation and to correct your mistakes. The karma of inactivity is much worse when under a plausible pretext you do not interfere in the fight, and you lose the won positions and the advantages of swiftness and inrush.

Do learn from your mistakes.

Do not hesitate to act for the benefit of the evolutions of planet Earth!

I AM El Morya!

You must return God into your life!

December 27, 2013

I AM El Morya!

Today I have come to you!

My dear chelas, beloved, every time my arrival becomes more and more sorrowful.

Yes, I must state the fact that many of my disciples, whom I laid my hopes on, have left the Path.

Illusion, its charm, led away from the Path many of the most devoted disciples of mine, who were with me throughout many incarnations.

And today I am stating this sorrowful fact.

What is to be done? Is it worth spreading panic and despair?

I will tell you that our assignments have not changed. Even having no superiority in numbers, we can manage to carry out these grandiose tasks!

Each of you, of my disciples, who are in embodiment, becomes as good as gold. Each of you is forced to struggle against the thousand-fold superior forces of the illusion.

Well, it is not the first time for you. Recall your incarnation with me in the days of King Arthur.

Your spirit of chivalry and devotion to God must be awakened!

I must tell you that not all the plans of the Masters are promoted the way that they were planned. We suffer one defeat after another and lose our most experienced warriors. This is sorrowful. But I invoke you always to go along the Supreme Path only!

Only if you constantly keep your consciousness focused on God, do you become invulnerable to the forces that oppose us.

Only your devotion to the Will of God! Only your determination to gain a victory! Only your desire to withstand!

I know that it is hard. I know that many have lost the Path. But I also know that the outcome of the battle between the Light and the dark is predetermined! I know that each devoted collaborator of the Brotherhood is able to resist the whole hordes of the forces of death and hell.

Knights of the Spirit! You are to unite before the crucial battles!

I say that you are to show all of your abilities and talents. You are to throw off everything that ties you to the illusion and its manifestations, both outside of you and inside of you.

Right now! Exactly at this time we are to withstand and create the overbalance of the forces at the crucial part of the battle! Therefore, I think, it's not worth going limp; do not panic.

It is necessary to draw up the battle formation and to aspire to our victory.

Yes, not all goes well. Yes, the majority is still on the side of the opposite forces.

However, we tirelessly repeat to you that the forces of Light will gain the Victory! For this is the Law of this Universe!

Every minute and every second of your embodiment you must be aware of your connection with God. Only in this case you get the invulnerable protection of the Light! Only in this case you will be able to advance towards your victory!

But if you weep and search for the causes of your failures outside of you, you will never gain the victory.

All the causes of your failures and defeats are inside you.

When your Faith becomes weaker, when you lose the connection with your Spirit, you become vulnerable to the opposite forces. The worm of doubt and sadness penetrates into your consciousness and inevitably brings the mood of defeat.

Therefore, do tirelessly bear your responsibility for the destiny of the world every day!

Every day, keep the victorious spirit and your devotion to God!

I know that the opposite forces use the craftiest methods. And I am telling you that your protection and your invulnerability are in the maintenance of your connection with God.

How many hours a day do you think about God?

How many days a week do you dedicate to your praying vigils?

How many days a year do you devote to the deeds for God and the Masters?

You must set in your bookkeeping records the time that you spare for God and the Masters in your life.

Then the cause of your defeats and failures will be clear for you.

Have I stated your forthcoming tasks clearly enough?

There is no excuse — and there cannot be any excuses — for your inactivity and laziness!

It is impossible to lie on the stove-bench when the enemy is conquering your land, your children and your family.

Everyone must fight the illusory forces like you are ten.

One can withstand the onslaught of a thousand if he is with God!

I will personally come and reinforce each of you who risk showing determination and resisting the illusory forces at this time, at the cost of his reputation and of his life.

Nothing matters in the situation that has formed on the Earth except for one thing — you must return God into your life! At any cost, even at the cost of your life.

I bless you for this feat of arms in the name of Life!

I AM El Morya!

Show your achievements and we will be ready to give you better understanding and more knowledge!

June 29, 2014

I AM El Morya!

< ... >

Thousands of people read our messages every day. Thousands of people located all over the world have an opportunity to get in touch with our energies and our Teaching.

However, where are these knights? Where are those deeds which you are called to fulfill?

Before the incarnation you have assumed certain obligations upon yourselves. Every time I come to remind you about what you have taken upon yourself.

And so what?

I see that your efforts are too small, and so we cannot successfully overcome the resistance of the forces opposite to us.

It is important for us to create the preponderance of our forces at every sector in the front of any sphere of human activity.

It is important for us that the numbers of people who aspire to follow the Teaching of the Ascended Masters and to practice this Teaching in their lives grow and increase from year to year.

It is exactly thanks to our sincere followers we can fulfill the plans of the Brotherhood for the given stage of the development of humanity!

That is why I come and tirelessly repeat that our tasks have not changed and our plans require fulfillment!

I remind you again and again that it is necessary to act!

How many of you who read our Messages have applied concrete efforts to fulfill our requests for the last half-year?

During this time we have held several very important initiatives through our Messenger.

How many of you supported these initiatives?

I will tell you that I am disappointed. We expected more, and our hopes have not been justified again.

Your inertness and laziness do no honor to you.

I understand very well that it is very hard to act and keep the Divine spirit in those circumstances that exist on the planet now.

However, I insist that you find the strength in yourselves to continue the advancement. I demand that all our chelas finally wake up from the lethargic sleep in the illusion and begin to implement our plans!

You should only overcome your own laziness and inertness. As soon as you make it you will be able to start perceiving our vibrations and our energies!

As soon as you become capable of perceiving our energies, you will find strength and desire to act, and nothing will ever be able to stop you on your Path to God!

I am telling you that you have to get out of the mustiness and perishables of the world around you!

I am telling you that for this, you must rouse yourself and start acting!

Your obstacles are lying in the sphere of your karmic problems. Only you, by your own effort, can disentangle your karmic obstacles.

First of all, you must wish to move along the Path shown by us.

For this, you need adamant faith and devotion.

These qualities are acquired by means of long and thorough work over yourself with the help of many hours of spiritual practices.

There are many ways to keep yourself constantly in the state of attunement with God. However, all of these tools require the application of your daily efforts.

Even one day cannot be missing. As soon as you miss one day of your spiritual practice, owing to your laziness or weakness, you roll back to the beginning of the Path and have to start your ascension again.

No excuses! No indulgence towards your own ego!

If you have taken the road of Serving the Brotherhood, you will have neither days off nor holidays!

Many are afraid of the discipline. Many think that the Masters demand too much.

I am clearly showing you the Path leading to the salvation of your soul. But I cannot surmount this Path for you.

You can choose. You do not have a wide choice; you either continue the evolution, or refuse the evolutionary path and choose decay and disintegration.

Very unfavorable tendencies begin to show in your world.

We apply all our efforts to support you and give you the last chance. All the instructions have been given for today! The Law does not allow giving more!

Show your achievements and we will be ready to give you better understanding and more knowledge!

Now I am saying goodbye to you.

And I hope to meet you again!

I AM El Morya!

I hope that my Message will light up the hearts of those who still have a sparkle of Divinity glowing inside!

June 21, 2015

I AM El Morya!

Urgency requires this Message to be strong or harsh.

We said that there was no opportunity to give more of our Messages through this Messenger.

It happened not because we did not wish for that or because the Messenger could not manage it.

We said that there was no opportunity to give our Messages because lots of the energy contained in our Messages was not in demand among you, our incarnated chelas.

We must state this fact with deep regret.

There is so much different information in your world.

There are so many different books and so much information scattered about different Internet pages.

But we do not come to give you information. We come in order for you return Home due to our help and the knowledge being given by us.

Your world, in this form that exists now, cannot satisfy the souls that remember the other world, the Divine World. These souls remember true relationships between people based on brotherly Love and Collaboration.

You, many of you, have lost that true and innermost ingredient of the heart of the Being.

No toys and pleasures of your world can replace that Truth, which is always with you, but which you forget in the hassle of the day.

I have come to remind those devoted hearts, which we have been connected with for numerous incarnations, of the Truth that resides in your hearts in the innermost of your being.

It becomes more and more difficult for the Ascended Hosts to reach out to your hearts covered with an impenetrable armor.

Few of the devoted and genuine who still remember God remain incarnated, and due to their devotion and great compassion toward humanity they are ready to sacrifice their very lives for the salvation of the souls of people who are lost in the illusory world and cannot see the Light.

For those few souls of Light, I come in order to support and help them despite the decision of the Karmic Board not to give any more Messages through our Messenger.

My compassion and desire to help humanity overcomes all obstacles and all difficulties.

I have come on this significant day, the Day of the summer solstice of 2015.

Today you can apply all your efforts and mentally change the situation on the planet for the better. Only a few light-bearers are required to keep the image of the bright future in their consciousness in order to clear away the darkness that is so saturated that people cannot distinguish the direction of their further movement.

All the energy in this Universe belongs to God.

God is the only One who in an instant can change any situation in the world.

Only the Law of free will granted to you by God does not allow positive changes in the world. Neither the Ascended Hosts nor God himself can help you if you turn away from the help and forget the name of God.

I remind you again and again: all your problems and all the problems of your society are connected with one thing only — your civilization separates itself from God.

It is in your power to get as much happiness, Love, and Divine Energy as your being can hold.

The only barrier is your karma, a negative energy, which lies between you and God and consists of your mistakes that you made in the past as a result of breaking the Law of this Universe.

For the last ten years we have been giving the Teaching that gives detailed recommendations on how you can overcome the mistakes of the past and gain the state of inner happiness and peace.

But now the time has come when you must show that our training is adopted by you.

You must show your aspiration and persistence in your spiritual practices.

You must demonstrate how our Messages, the given dispensations and opportunities are adopted by you.

All that you need at this stage for your salvation is given to you in full!

If it is beyond your power to adopt the Teaching given by us, appeal directly to God and the Masters. Ask for help, ask for liberation, and help will come!

But if you still sit idly and hope for a miracle, you are risking too much, as the time is short and this time is the last time.

I hope that my Message will light up the hearts of those who still have a sparkle of Divinity glowing inside!

I AM El Morya!

Right now it is the time for your work for the good of the evolutions of planet Earth!

December 23, 2015

I AM Master Morya! Now, I have come to you today, my beloved chelas.

I understand very well that the black clouds have gathered and how hard it is for you now to endure the pressure of the forces opposing Us.

It would seem that there is nothing joyful and positive. However, I have come to assure you that, on the contrary, there is a reason to rejoice and a cause to celebrate!

We have had long conversations with you, and We have been giving Our Teaching.

At last, for those few who were able to absorb Our Teaching in its fullest, it is exactly the period of time that we have prepared you for, not only in these long 10 years when we have been giving the Teaching through our Messenger. Of course not. You were preparing for this work of yours in many of your incarnations.

We have repeatedly said that now the best of our disciples are incarnated. This is due to the harshness of the time and the intensity of the battle between the Light and the dark.

And now, the decisive stage has come for you!

All that we have been doing before is just the groundwork.

The two forces clash in the global battle for the future of mankind: the forces defending the illusion and the forces wishing mankind to return Home to God.

When the forces are strained, when each party brings to bear all its power, a period of chaos arrives when everything is mixed up, and it becomes almost impossible to discern who acts on which side.

And your turn comes in this period of chaos.

The opposite forces use rough methods of Influence, brute physical force, and haunting patterns and stereotypes.

However, the most cunning and dodgy understand that the more brute force that they apply, the stronger is the probability for them to be ruined under the impact of these forces. That is why they use more subtle methods, by influencing the consciousness and the unconsciousness of the masses to adopt the states of fear, aggression, hatred, and hostility.

Beloved, all of these states cannot have any continuation in the New world.

The world is on the threshold of the New Age. It will be coming inevitably, exactly as the sun rises at the end of a night, no matter how dark it was.

At this time, each of you, our devoted chelas, becomes indispensable, because at this time of chaos it is exactly the slight impacts that have the strongest influence.

I will give you an example of a doctor who uses the method of acupuncture.

Imagine a patient suffering from a serious disease. However, if the doctor is highly qualified, one slight impact of a thin needle is enough to improve the state of a patient. And several such impacts can cure the patient completely.

Our devoted disciples have the skills that allow them to keep the inner balance of energies within them, no matter what the outer chaos is around them.

Thus, they represent the conductors of Our most subtle energies coming into this world, and this can change the world situation.

We have our disciples in every country. Through them we can influence the situation in the world.

We are glad that the time has come when we can use this reserve of ours. Exactly now it is the time when only by the inner power of the few, the situation in the world can be changed at the global level.

Well, I wish you good luck!

Always remember that the outer is determined by the inner. Thus, if a sufficient number of individuals can manage to maintain inner peace and harmony, the feelings of joy and love in any outer chaos, then the situation in the world can change for the better literally within a few years.

However, never forget that in the state of chaos, the situation can quickly worsen as well.

Therefore, you must not relax! Your complete readiness is needed! Complete concentration on the Supreme.

The inner determines the outer.

Right now it is the time for your work for the good of the evolutions of planet Earth! Only inner balance, even if the whole world collapses.

None of the souls that have chosen the Divine Path can be lost!

As soon as you make your choice in favor of God, all the Ascended Hosts stand up to protect your soul, no matter what the external circumstances are.

Therefore, remember God every moment of your life and devote your entire life to God and to fulfilling His Law!

I AM Morya!

...You can use my focus, my image, and every day address me with your requests and problems, your questions and wishes.

The divisibility of my consciousness and the opportunity given to me by God allow me to be present in many places simultaneously and to give you my directions and recommendations.

I hear all of you, who address me. Only you have to learn to hear me. I come to you and speak from the silence of your heart. Try to hear me.

El Morya
July 19, 2006

ABOUT THE AUTHOR

Tatyana Nicholaevna Mickushina was born in the south of western Siberia in the town of Omsk. During all of her life, she has been praying and asking God to grant her an opportunity to work for Him.

In 2004, Tatyana N. Mickushina was granted a Messenger's Mantle of the Great White Brotherhood and received an opportunity to bring the Words of the Masters to people. Since 2005, at certain periods of time, she receives messages from the Ascended Masters in a special way. With the help of many people, the messages have been translated into English and many other languages so that more people can become familiar with them.

"The only thing the Ascended Masters want is to spread their Teaching throughout the world.

The Masters give their messages with the feeling of great Love. Love has no limits.

There are no boundaries between the hearts of people living in different countries; there are no boundaries between the worlds. The boundaries exist only in the consciousness of people.

The Masters appeal through me to every person living on planet Earth.

I wish you success on the spiritual Path!"

Light and Love!
Tatyana Mickushina

BOOKS BY
TATYANA N. MICKUSHINA

WORDS OF WISDOM SERIES

The "Words of Wisdom" series of books was created based on the Ascended Masters' Messages that have been given through T.N. Mickushina. Since 2005, she has received over 450 Messages from more than 50 Beings of Light. You can find the Dictations on the website "Sirius" **sirius-eng.net** (English version) and **sirius-ru.net** or **sirius-net.org** (Russian version).

The Ascended Masters have been communicating with mankind for thousands of years. Since ancient times, the Masters of Shambala were known in the East. In different teachings, people call them by different names: the Teachers of Humanity, the Ascended Masters, the Masters of Wisdom or the Great White Brotherhood.

These Teachers have reached the next evolutionary step in their development and continue their development in the Higher planes. These Higher Beings consider it Their duty to help humanity in the development of their consciousness.

The method which the Ascended Masters have chosen to communicate with humanity is the transmission of the Messages (Dictations) that are written by the Messenger who can use a special method to provide the perception of the Messages from the higher, etheric octaves of Light.

238

Words of Wisdom

The first Dictation from Sanat Kumara on March 4, 2005, gave us the following message:

"I AM Sanat Kumara and I have come today to inform the world about a new opportunity and a new dispensation which the Heavens have decided to free through our new Russian Messenger Tatyana.

This turn of events will be unexpected for many of you. Many of you will experience contradictory feelings while reading this message.

However, we do not want to force anybody to believe or not to believe the things to be told. Our task is to give you this knowledge. Its acceptance is a matter of your own free will.

Times have changed and the New Age has come. The worlds have converged. Things which seemed to be an impossible dream a few years ago, even last year, are starting to become real now. We are getting an opportunity to speak through many of you and we are using this opportunity."

BOOKS BY
TATYANA N. MICKUSHINA

MASTERS OF WISDOM SERIES

Each of the Masters of Wisdom strives to give us what they consider most vital at the present moment of transition. Every message contains the energies of different Masters who give those messages. The Masters speak about the current historical moment on planet Earth. They tell us about energy and vibrations, about the illusion of this world and about the Divine Reality, about the Higher Self of a human and about his lower bodies. They give us concrete recommendations on exactly how to change our own consciousness and continue on the evolutionary Path. It is recommended that you prepare yourself for reading every message very carefully. You have to tune to the Master who is giving the message with the help of proper music, with the help of the Master's image, or by using a prayer or a meditation before reading the message. That way you align your energies, elevate your consciousness, and the messages can benefit you.

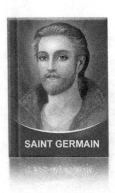

SAINT GERMAIN

SAINT GERMAIN

Saint Germain is at present an Ascended Master, the Hierarch of the New Age. In his last incarnation as the Count de Saint Germain in the 18th century, he exerted a great influence on the course of world history. The Messages of Master Saint Germain are charged with optimism and faith in the forthcoming Golden Age! He teaches about preparing for a New Age by transforming our consciousness, and reminds us: "Joy and Love come to you when your Faith is steadfast, when you rely in your consciousness on God and the Ascended Hosts."

SANAT KUMARA

SANAT KUMARA

Masters of Wisdom, first of all Sanat Kumara, remind us about our Divine origin and call us to wake up to a Higher reality, because Divine Reality by its love, wisdom, and beauty exceeds any of the most wonderful aspects of our physical world. The Messages of Sanat Kumara include Teachings on true and false messengers, Communities of the Holy Spirit, responsibility for the duties that one has taken upon him/herself before their incarnation, the right use of the money energy, the choice of everyone between the Eternal and the perishable world, overcoming the ego, the Path of Initiations, and many other topics.

Author page of T. N. Mickushina on Amazon:

amazon.com/author/tatyana_mickushina

Masters of Wisdom

MORYA

**Dictations received through the Messenger
Tatyana Nicholaevna Mickushina
from 2005 through 2015**

Tatyana N. Mickushina

Websites:

http://sirius-eng.net (English version)
http://sirius-ru.net (Russian version)

Books by T.N.Mickushina on amazon.com:
amazon.com/author/tatyana_mickushina

CPSIA information can be obtained
at www.ICGtesting.com
Printed in the USA
FSHW020054260819
61412FS